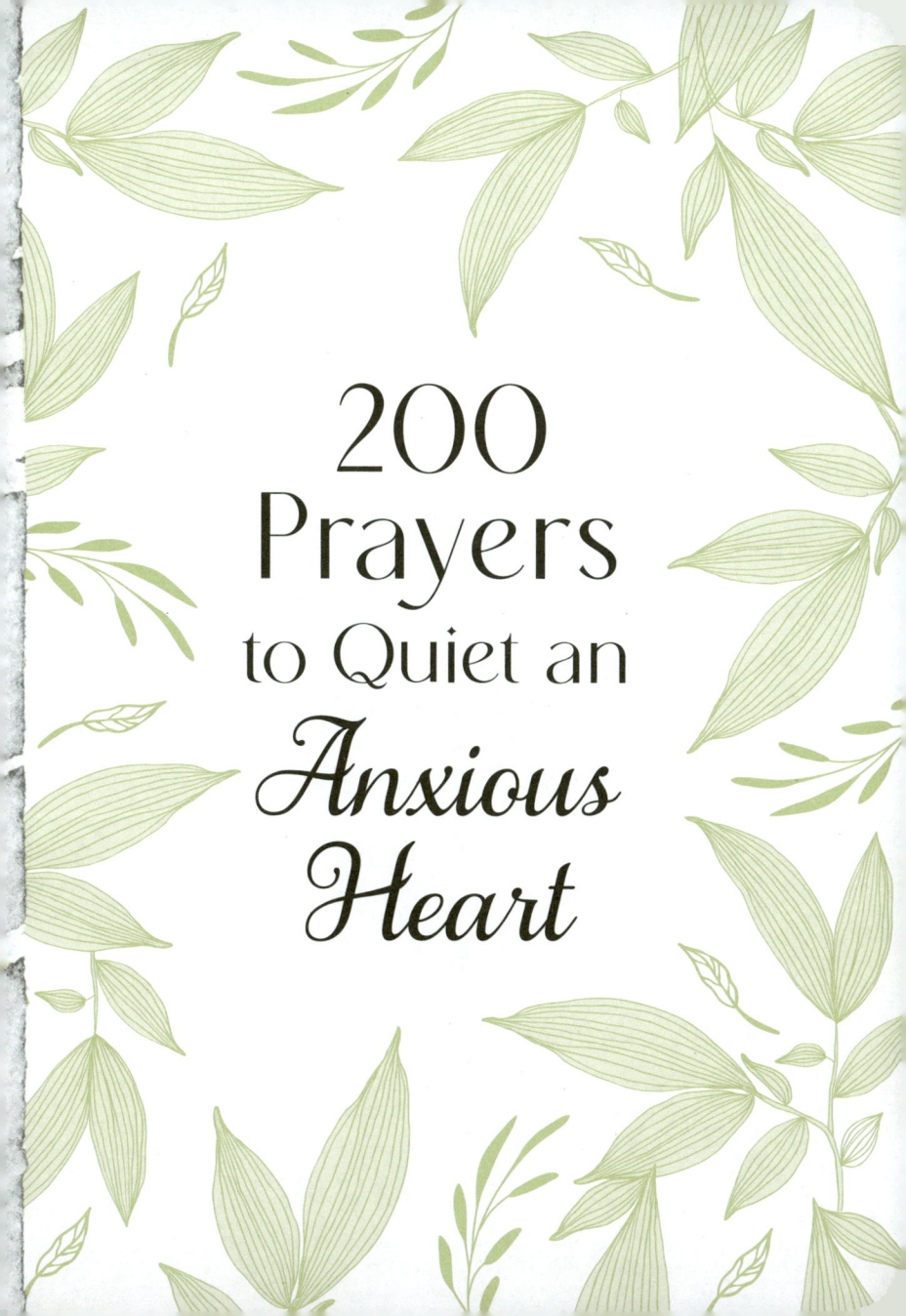

Carey Scott

200 Prayers to Quiet an *Anxious Heart*

Peace and Comfort *for* Women

BARBOUR
PUBLISHING

© 2024 by Barbour Publishing, Inc.

Print ISBN 978-1-63609-874-6

Some text previously published in *99 Prayers for When You Feel Alone*, published by Barbour Publishing, Inc.

All rights reserved. No part of this publication may be reproduced or transmitted for commercial purposes, except for brief quotations in printed reviews, without written permission of the publisher. Reproduced text may not be used on the World Wide Web.

Churches and other noncommercial interests may reproduce portions of this book without the express written permission of Barbour Publishing, provided that the text does not exceed 500 words or 5 percent of the entire book, whichever is less, and that the text is not from material quoted from another publisher. When reproducing text from this book, include the following credit line: "From *200 Prayers to Quiet an Anxious Heart*, published by Barbour Publishing, Inc. Used by permission."

Scripture quotations marked msg are from *THE MESSAGE*. Copyright © by Eugene H. Peterson 1993, 1994, 1995, 1996, 2000, 2001, 2002. Used by permission of NavPress Publishing Group.

Scripture quotations marked ampc are taken from the Amplified® Bible, Classic Edition, Copyright © 1954, 1958, 1962, 1964, 1965, 1987 by The Lockman Foundation. Used by permission.

Scripture quotations marked amp are taken from the Amplified® Bible, © 1954, 1958, 1962, 1964, 1965, 1987 by The Lockman Foundation. Used by permission.

Scripture quotations marked ceb are taken from the Common English Bible® Copyright © 2010, 2011 by Common English Bible,™ Used by permission.

Scripture quotations marked nlt are taken from the *Holy Bible*. New Living Translation copyright© 1996, 2004, 2015 by Tyndale House Foundation. Used by permission of Tyndale House Publishers, Inc. Carol Stream, Illinois 60188. All rights reserved.

Scripture quotations marked voice are taken from The Voice™. Copyright © 2008 by Ecclesia Bible Society. Used by permission. All rights reserved.

Published by Barbour Publishing, Inc., 1810 Barbour Drive, Uhrichsville, Ohio 44683, www.barbourbooks.com

Our mission is to inspire the world with the life-changing message of the Bible.

Printed in China.

Introduction

Everyone battles with anxious feelings from time to time. It's part of the human condition that knits us together. But when those feelings become overwhelming, what you do next can make a big difference.

God's constant message is to trust His hand in your life. He promises to never leave nor forsake you, thereby making you brave and confident to live and love well. Let this book be a guide as you talk to the Lord about the condition of your heart and receive His encouragement.

Remember that fear and worry are Satan's tools to paralyze so you become ineffective in your Christian walk. But God has lots to say on these topics, and He promises to meet You in the Word and the pages of this book to strengthen your resolve as you stand strong.

When anxiety overtakes me and worries are many,
Your comfort lightens my soul.
PSALM 94:19 VOICE

1
No Benefit to Worry

God, I don't want to spend my time obsessing over what might be. Remind me that worry doesn't help in any way. So let me trust You for peace in every moment. You're the only one who can bring a sense of calm to my heart in meaningful ways.

*"Who among you by worrying can add
a single moment to your life?"*
MATTHEW 6:27 CEB

2
He Will Take You In

God, pull me in close to You and take this empty feeling away from me! I feel hopeless and unwanted, and I'm desperate to know that I matter. Speak kindly into my heart and remind me that I am important in Your eyes. I need to know that right now.

> *Even if my father and mother abandon*
> *me, the L ORD will hold me close.*
> PSALM 27:10 NLT

3
Let Him Carry It

God, what a gift to know I'm welcome to offload to You the things that weigh heavily on my heart. Now give me the courage to do so. Let me be quick to release stress into Your capable arms. And allow me to embrace the freedom that comes with it!

*Since God cares for you, let Him carry
all your burdens and worries.*
1 PETER 5:7 VOICE

4
Kicked in the Gut

God, meet me right where I am in my sadness. I'm feeling tossed aside and uncared for and my heart is broken. I never saw this level of betrayal coming and I'm at a loss. Restore my peace and hope like only You can.

If your heart is broken,
*you'll find G*od *right there;*
if you're kicked in the gut,
he'll help you catch your breath.
PSALM 34:18 MSG

5
Instead, Pray

God, sometimes my worry becomes so overwhelming that I forget to pray about it. I'm too busy trying to work it all out and forget You're all I need to find peace. Your presence is what will settle my heart so I can find my footing again. Today, will You displace the worry sitting at the center of my life? Will You surround me with love so my heart can be at peace?

Don't fret or worry. Instead of worrying, pray. Let petitions and praises shape your worries into prayers, letting God know your concerns. Before you know it, a sense of God's wholeness, everything coming together for good, will come and settle you down. It's wonderful what happens when Christ displaces worry at the center of your life.
Philippians 4:6–7 msg

6
Lonely from Loss

God, my heart grieves the loss of my husband. For so many years, he was my closest friend and companion and I'm missing him so much right now. Please comfort my broken heart, and please fill the empty space with Your holy presence. I need You right now!

Two are better than one because a good return comes when two work together. If one of them falls, the other can help him up. But who will help the pitiful person who falls down alone?
ECCLESIASTES 4:9–10 VOICE

7
My Source

God, You promise to meet my every need—the spiritual and emotional ones as well as the physical ones. Scripture reveals that You are my source! You are my caring Father who will provide. Forgive me for the times I forget this and spend my day focused on what I lack instead of Your love for me. Increase my faith so that I'm unshakable. And open my eyes to see the abundance of Your goodness in my life.

"Therefore I tell you, stop being worried or anxious (perpetually uneasy, distracted) about your life, as to what you will eat or what you will drink; nor about your body, as to what you will wear. Is life not more than food, and the body more than clothing?"
MATTHEW 6:25 AMP

8
Alone through Illness

God, I am holding hope that I will be reunited with my family and friends soon. This illness has been a hard and lonely road and I'm missing my community. While I understand the need for temporary separation, I am so lonely. Please reunite us as soon as possible.

Build up hope so you'll all be together in this, no one left out, no one left behind. I know you're already doing this; just keep on doing it.
1 Thessalonians 5:11 msg

9
The Red Flag of Lingering Sadness

God, if I begin to experience any lingering sadness or depression, let it be a red flag that there may be some unchecked fear I'm feeling inside. Your Word tells me anxiety can bring this on. And in those moments, remind me to seek encouragement through scripture or through friends and family who love me. Sometimes their kindness can ease my worry and bring forth joy in the most powerful and precious ways.

*Worry weighs a person down;
an encouraging word cheers a person up.*
PROVERBS 12:25 NLT

10
The Wise Friend

God, help me be the kind of woman to welcome wise counsel from a friend. I have been too quick to dismiss their care and it's broken our trust. Teach me to value community so I don't walk through life alone.

The heart is delighted by the fragrance of oil and sweet perfumes, and in just the same way, the soul is sweetened by the wise counsel of a friend.
PROVERBS 27:9 VOICE

11
God's Perfect Peace

God, what a blessing to realize Your peace is perfect. It's unmatched in all the world. And no matter what others may offer or suggest, there is no remedy as perfect as what You promise to provide to my anxious heart. Give me courage to trust You in every stressful situation and chaotic circumstance, especially knowing that when I do Your peace will bring balance and courage when I need it most.

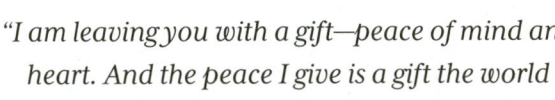

"I am leaving you with a gift—peace of mind and heart. And the peace I give is a gift the world cannot give. So don't be troubled or afraid."
JOHN 14:27 NLT

12
He Will Never Turn Away from You

God, I know that even when it feels like You aren't there, You are. Even when it seems my prayers are bouncing off the ceiling, they aren't. Bolster my confidence to know there is nothing that will make You turn from me. You'll never leave me to be alone.

*At three, Jesus cried out with a loud shout,
"Eloi, eloi, lama sabachthani," which means,
"My God, my God, why have you left me?"*
MARK 15:34 CEB

13
Your Entire Attention

God, I want to give You my full attention so I can keep perspective on what's happening. When I do, it means my eyes are focused on Your goodness rather than my gravities. My thoughts are on Your promises and not my pressures. And my heart is unshaken by anxiety because You are unmatched in authority. I know You will help me deal with every hard thing in the right time. Help me trust You always.

"Give your entire attention to what God is doing right now, and don't get worked up about what may or may not happen tomorrow. God will help you deal with whatever hard things come up when the time comes."
MATTHEW 6:34 MSG

14
The Need to Connect with Others

God, when I'm embarrassed about myself and feel exposed, I hide away. It just feels safer to be alone. But honestly, community is so good for my heart and I don't want to push it away. Please boost my confidence, remind me I don't have to be perfect, and encourage me to reach out and connect.

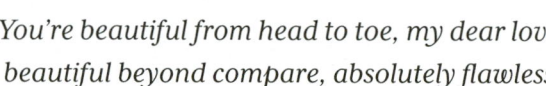

You're beautiful from head to toe, my dear love, beautiful beyond compare, absolutely flawless.
SONG OF SOLOMON 4:7 MSG

15
Strengthened by God

God, for me to be content, I must also be at peace. When I'm full of worry and stress, my spirit is unsettled and I'm anything but comfortable. I feel a sense of hopelessness that bleeds into every area of my life. And it shuts me down. But in those anxious moments, remind me I can ask You to strengthen me for the situation. You're my power and peace that allows me to stand strong.

I can be content in any and every situation through the Anointed One who is my power and strength.
PHILIPPIANS 4:13 VOICE

16
Loneliness from Keeping Up

God, it's lonely trying to keep up with the Joneses. Watching my friends purchase new cars, take expensive trips, and fill their homes with the latest and greatest reminds me that I can't keep up. So rather than try, I hide away in shame. Your Word says any treasures on earth are worthless and heavenly stockpiles should be my focus. That means it's okay if I can't keep up with others. I'm not supposed to!

"Don't hoard treasure down here where it gets eaten by moths and corroded by rust or—worse!—stolen by burglars. Stockpile treasure in heaven, where it's safe from moth and rust and burglars. It's obvious, isn't it? The place where your treasure is, is the place you will most want to be, and end up being."
MATTHEW 6:19–21 MSG

17
A Refreshing Oasis

God, my heart is heavy with worry today. I feel upset and uneasy deep in my bones. Hear my cries, Father, and bring refreshment to my soul. Give me an eternal perspective so I can stand strong in my faith, knowing You are in control. Be an oasis in the desert of disappointment. And remove the weight on my shoulders so I can stand tall in the freedom Jesus came to bring.

*Come to Me, all who are weary and
burdened, and I will give you rest.*
MATTHEW 11:28 VOICE

18
Hiding Place

God, I'm feeling attacked from all sides and standing alone without anyone to protect me. It's hard to speak up to advocate for my needs, especially when it seems no one cares. Thanks for hiding me from harm and reminding me of my freedom.

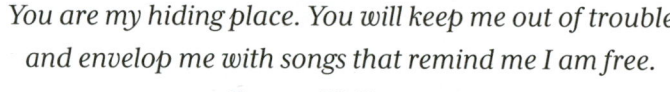

You are my hiding place. You will keep me out of trouble and envelop me with songs that remind me I am free.
Psalm 32:7 voice

19
Distracted by Needs

God, I confess there are times I'm distracted by my needs. And rather than take those worries to You, I take matters into my own hands. Comfort me today and remind me that there is no reason to worry for You are with me always.

"Therefore do not worry or be anxious (perpetually uneasy, distracted), saying, 'What are we going to eat?' or 'What are we going to drink?' or 'What are we going to wear?'. . . for your heavenly Father knows that you need them."
MATTHEW 6:31–32 AMP

20
When the Problem Is You

God, maybe the reason I struggle with community is because I'm not living out today's verse in my everyday life. Maybe I am expecting to be treated one way but not treating others the same way. Father, open my eyes to the places where I am bringing about my own loneliness. Show me where I need to make changes. Help me see the ways I'm not living and loving others well. I am listening!

If you don't want to be judged, don't judge.
If you don't want to be condemned, don't
condemn. If you want to be forgiven, forgive.
LUKE 6:37 VOICE

21
Be Consistently Righteous

God, Your Word tells me that when I am consistent in my pursuit of righteous living, You won't let me fall. Every anxious thought won't be allowed to take root. And even more, You will sustain me as You lovingly take my burdens. What a great reminder to pursue faith every day.

Cast your burden on the Lord [releasing the weight of it] and He will sustain you.
PSALM 55:22 AMPC

22
When Family Rejects

God, family is messy. And there are so many strings attached that it's easy to get tangled in expectations I can't or won't meet. Standing up for my faith often means alienation by the ones I always thought would be there for me. But none of this escapes You. In my abandonment and rejection, I know You'll be my companion. Bring other faith-honoring friends to fill the emptiness too. I trust You to meet every need!

Your own parents, brothers, relatives, and friends will turn on you and turn you in. Some of you will be killed, and all of you will be hated by everyone for the sake of My name.
Luke 21:16–17 voice

23
There Is Nothing to Fear

God, I'm learning just how powerful Your presence is. Scripture says there's nothing to fear because of it. I don't have to let my circumstances fuel any distress or dismay because I am Yours. And instead of giving up or giving in to worry, I can trust You to strengthen me. You'll straighten my spine, so I stand tall in truth. And victory over it all will be mine through You!

Fear not [there is nothing to fear], for I am with you; do not look around you in terror and be dismayed, for I am your God. I will strengthen and harden you to difficulties, yes, I will help you; yes, I will hold you up and retain you with My [victorious] right hand of rightness and justice.
Isaiah 41:10 ampc

24
God Will Meet You

God, I feel mismatched in some of my relationships right now. There's a tension between what I know are healthy thoughts and what I'm being pressured to believe. I'm struggling with how to stand strong in truth because I'm afraid of abandonment if I go against their ideas. Please encourage my heart to stay true to Your Word, trusting that You will honor it. I don't want to be alone, but I know You'll meet me in my loneliness.

Don't team up with those who are unbelievers. How can righteousness be a partner with wickedness? How can light live with darkness? What harmony can there be between Christ and the devil? How can a believer be a partner with an unbeliever?
2 Corinthians 6:14–15 nlt

25
Generously Supply

God, I need a big dose of confidence today. I've been stressed out by what's ahead, and it's made me feel too weak to move forward. I feel ill equipped. All my fears are rushing at me. I'm timid and nervous, unsure how best to proceed. I do believe You will generously supply me with everything I need, according to Your perfect will and timing. Bolster my anxious heart with that beautiful truth today!

And my God will liberally supply (fill until full) your every need according to His riches in glory in Christ Jesus.
Philippians 4:19 amp

26
Self-Made Loneliness

God, open my eyes to see the needs of others rather than self-isolating as I fixate on my tough circumstances. Sometimes the desire to protect my own heart keeps me alone and missing out of community. Help me trust You with my brokenness so I'm still able to contribute to relationships around me in meaningful ways. I want to be ready and able to bless others rather than get locked up in my self-made prison of selfishness.

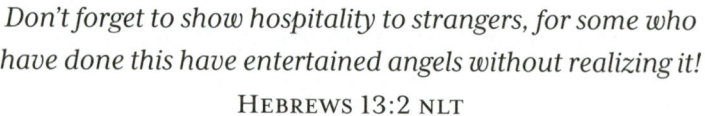

Don't forget to show hospitality to strangers, for some who have done this have entertained angels without realizing it!
HEBREWS 13:2 NLT

27
When I Need Refreshment

God, when I find myself weighted with worry, I crave calm. I hunger after quietness in my spirit. I pine for peace, the kind only You can give me. And then I remember that when I press in and transfer my worries to You, I will find refreshment and rest. All that I long for will be found in Your compassion. Thank You for knowing my needs and meeting them in meaningful ways.

"Take my yoke upon you. Let me teach you, because I am humble and gentle at heart, and you will find rest for your souls. For my yoke is easy to bear, and the burden I give you is light."
MATTHEW 11:29–30 NLT

28
Walking Away

God, give me the courage to walk away from the bad influences in my life. Too often, I justify staying with them because I fear loneliness more. Help me trust that You will meet my need for belonging in the perfect ways, and that my obedience will not go unnoticed. You know my fears and insecurities, and I'm trusting that You will untangle them so I can find community in all the right places.

Walk away from the company of fools,
for you cannot find insight in their words.
PROVERBS 14:7 VOICE

29
Believe Confidently

God, help me believe confidently in Your willingness and ability to settle my anxious heart. If I begin to doubt, remind me of Your promise to bring comfort when I'm stirred up. You are unfailingly reliable. Trusting in You allows me to find rest from the fears and worries that keep me up at night and disrupt my days. I will hold on to You as I wait for peace to flood into my heart.

"Do not let your heart be troubled (afraid, cowardly). Believe [confidently] in God and trust in Him, [have faith, hold on to it, rely on it, keep going and] believe also in Me."
JOHN 14:1 AMP

30
Whose Opinion Matters Most?

God, mature my faith so I'm able to trust who You say I am more than worrying about what others think. When I focus my attention on worldly opinions, I'm stirred up. But when I find rest in Your thoughts about me, I'm content and at peace. Give me confidence to be alone when it's the right thing to do. And when it's time, give me courage to seek community with the right people.

*The fear of human opinion disables;
trusting in God protects you from that.*
PROVERBS 29:25 MSG

31
A Stabilizing Force

God, Your Word is clear when it tells me to live with strength and courage. Scripture says I shouldn't allow fear or discouragement to guide me. But today, I find myself overwhelmed with worry and unable to shake it. Remind me that we take every step together because Your presence never leaves. It's a stabilizing force. And when I surrender each burden, I will receive the powerful peace that comes from choosing faith over fear.

"Haven't I commanded you? Strength! Courage! Don't be timid; don't get discouraged. God, your God, is with you every step you take."
JOSHUA 1:9 MSG

32
Because Jesus Understands

God, Your Son understands the lonely feelings better than anyone. He knows what it's like to be despised and abandoned. Jesus felt rejection. And as hard as it is to imagine Him walking this out, I deeply appreciate how relatable it makes Him. When I cry out in anguish with these same issues, it matters so much that Jesus understands. It encourages me to know that He will comfort me through them.

So he was despised and forsaken by men, this man of suffering, grief's patient friend. As if he was a person to avoid, we looked the other way; he was despised, forsaken, and we took no notice of him.
ISAIAH 53:3 VOICE

33
Nothing Is Impossible

God, sometimes it feels hopeless for me to give up the habit of worrying day in and day out. I've been apprehensive most of my life. Even more, it's a generational curse passed down in my family. I come from a long line of worriers. But then I read that, through You, nothing is ever impossible—and that truth restores hope for a peaceful heart. Would You make it so today? I could really use encouragement right now.

For with God nothing is ever impossible and no word from God shall be without power or impossible of fulfillment.
LUKE 1:37 AMPC

34
The Company You Keep

God, I know the company I keep matters. They can either be beneficial, helping me grow and mature to become the best version possible; or they can influence me negatively and cause me to make wrong choices that lead me away from You. Help me make the hard decisions even if that means my community may be limited, and at times leave me feeling lonely. I trust You to fill those empty spaces.

Walk with the wise and become wise;
associate with fools and get in trouble.
PROVERBS 13:20 NLT

35
God's Perfect Love

God, today I'm worried about retaliation. I am concerned that by standing up and advocating for myself, I created a setup for retribution. Rather than sit and worry about what may be, let me soak in Your perfect love. Bring comfort to my heart as I trust You to straighten out the crooked path. I don't need to fear anything or anyone. Instead, I can stand strong in my faith knowing that I am covered by Your goodness.

Such love has no fear, because perfect love expels all fear. If we are afraid, it is for fear of punishment, and this shows that we have not fully experienced his perfect love.
1 JOHN 4:18 NLT

36
God Fully Knows You

God, in those times I feel unknown, bring me back to today's verse that clearly states You've known me since before I took my first breath. Before I saw the light of day I was fully known, and my future plans had been established. You have never left my side, not for one moment. I may feel alone but the reality is that I am not. Thank You for being my constant companion, invested in my life!

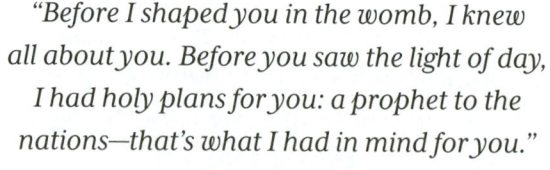

"Before I shaped you in the womb, I knew all about you. Before you saw the light of day, I had holy plans for you: a prophet to the nations—that's what I had in mind for you."
JEREMIAH 1:5 MSG

37
The God of Possible

God, there are days I'm acutely aware of my humanity. I feel inadequate and unable to take the next step in my situation, creating a wallop of worries that whisper lies into my heart. They tell me that I can't. They remind me of the times I tried and failed. And as I look down the road, I only see terrible outcomes and horrible endings. But today, I can be brave knowing nothing is impossible for You.

"Nothing is impossible for God."
LUKE 1:37 CEB

38
Expecting Lonely Seasons

God, it helps knowing I should expect some lonely seasons. I don't want to live on the world's terms, striving for its acceptance. Instead, I want my life to reflect a relationship with Jesus. I want my words and actions to point to You in heaven. And if that means I may find myself struggling to find community every now and then, help me remember that You promise to never leave me nor forsake me.

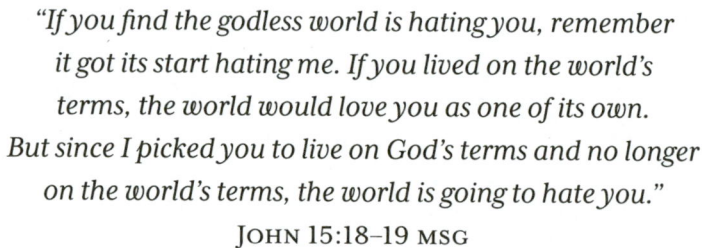

"If you find the godless world is hating you, remember it got its start hating me. If you lived on the world's terms, the world would love you as one of its own. But since I picked you to live on God's terms and no longer on the world's terms, the world is going to hate you."
JOHN 15:18–19 MSG

39
When I Let God Lead

God, I confess the times I've relied on my own opinions and trusted in my own ways, ending up full of worry and fear. The truth is I simply don't have all the key details to make the best decisions. But Father, You do. Today, help me rely only on Your guidance for my next steps. Give me an extra measure of faith so I can surrender in confidence to Your leading.

Trust in the Lord with all your heart; do not depend on your own understanding. Seek his will in all you do, and he will show you which path to take.
Proverbs 3:5–6 nlt

40
The Pitfall of Approval

God, empower me not to care so much about pleasing people that I go against what I know is true and right. In my pursuit of community, don't allow me to lose my moral compass. I don't want those lonely feelings to cause me to make the wrong choices for the approval of others. I would rather stand alone for a season with You than sacrifice our relationship to feel accepted by the wrong people. Please give me wisdom.

Do you think I care about the approval of men or about the approval of God? Do you think I am on a mission to please people? If I am still spinning my wheels trying to please men, then there is no way I can be a servant of the Anointed One, the Liberating King.
GALATIANS 1:10 VOICE

41
His Great Generosity

God, I'm feeling unusually overwhelmed with anxious thoughts and fear-filled considerations. I'm unsettled, and everything feels chaotic. In Your great generosity, please give me rest as I meditate on Your goodness.

When anxiety overtakes me and worries are many, Your comfort lightens my soul.
PSALM 94:19 VOICE

42
Sin Keeps You Alone

God, thank You for freedom. Thank You for removing the chains of bondage that keep me in sin and slavery. And thank You for calling me to stand my ground. It's always a telltale sign that I'm falling back into the yoke of slavery when I choose to isolate myself from others. Open my eyes to see that tendency because so often I'm not aware I'm headed there. Sin keeps me alone. Freedom invites community.

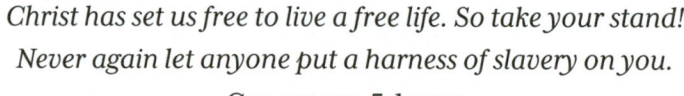

Christ has set us free to live a free life. So take your stand! Never again let anyone put a harness of slavery on you.
GALATIANS 5:1 MSG

43
God Knows What He's Doing

God, what a relief to know You are in control and have perfect plans for my life. Build my confidence through faith so I can rest in You rather than strive on my own.

"I know what I'm doing. I have it all planned out—plans to take care of you, not abandon you, plans to give you the future you hope for."
Jeremiah 29:11 msg

44
God Always Notices

God, my heart is blessed to know that You come looking for those You love. Sometimes I wonder if anyone notices I am not around. Does anyone see that I'm not out and about? Am I missed? Thank You for adding this verse to Your Word because it encourages me to know that You will always notice when I'm hiding. And even more, You will come looking for me because I matter to You.

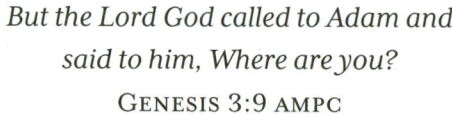

But the Lord God called to Adam and said to him, Where are you?
GENESIS 3:9 AMPC

45
Believing, Trusting, Relying

God, help me be the kind of woman who believes in, trusts in, and relies on You for confidence. Let me sink every hope into Your powerful promise to be my source for all things. It's only through You that I am able to reject the temptation of worry. It's by faith that I can refuse to partner with anxious thoughts. Thank You for being accessible through prayer 24/7, especially in those moments when I feel ill equipped in the battle for peace.

*[Most] blessed is the man who believes in,
trusts in, and relies on the Lord, and whose
hope and confidence the Lord is.*
JEREMIAH 17:7 AMPC

46
The Holy Spirit

God, how can I feel alone when I realize I have the Holy Spirit living in me? Because I've accepted Jesus as my Savior, Your Spirit has now taken up residence in my body. I have a built-in friend 24/7 who promises to never leave. The Spirit is alive and active, guiding me and empowering me to live a righteous life. Let me remember His presence anytime I begin to feel lonely.

Don't you realize that your body is the temple of the Holy Spirit, who lives in you and was given to you by God? You do not belong to yourself.
1 Corinthians 6:19 nlt

47
Deep Roots

God, rather than allowing myself to break down under the weight of worry, I want to stand firm regardless of what threatens to shake me. I want my belief in Your goodness to prevail. And I don't want any intimidating circumstance to rattle my faith. Help me grow deep roots so I am firmly secure when worrisome moments come my way. I know You will deliver me from every one of them.

They will be like trees planted by the streams, whose roots reach down to the water. They won't fear drought when it comes; their leaves will remain green. They won't be stressed in the time of drought or fail to bear fruit.
JEREMIAH 17:8 CEB

48
Asking God to Uncover

God, would You search me and let me know if I am doing something to alienate others? Would You look at my heart and motives and uncover anything in me that needs readjustment? This isn't the first time I've found myself in this lonely place, and I am open to Your correction if necessary. Sharpen my eyes and ears to the truth. And give me the courage to make any changes You may reveal.

Explore me, O God, and know the real me. Dig deeply and discover who I am. Put me to the test and watch how I handle the strain. Examine me to see if there is an evil bone in me, and guide me down Your path forever.
PSALM 139:23–24 VOICE

49
The Shepherd's Calm

God, there are times I feel as though I just need to catch my breath. When the world feels chaotic and destabilizing, it's hard to stop my heart from racing. And too often, my emotions begin to spiral as I shut down. Help me remember that You are my Shepherd. You are the one who steadies me in those moments. And when I run to You, I will find safety and comfort in Your presence.

God, my shepherd! I don't need a thing. You have bedded me down in lush meadows, you find me quiet pools to drink from. True to your word, you let me catch my breath and send me in the right direction.
Psalm 23:1–3 msg

50
Never Unseen

God, anytime I feel unseen let me remember that You know the smallest of details about me. Let me remember that I'm a one-of-a-kind creation. Remind me that I was made on purpose and for a purpose, and that You don't make trash. Fill my heart with the knowledge of how much I mean to You. And open my eyes to the truth that You're always with me as I navigate the ups and downs of this life.

I will offer You my grateful heart, for I am Your unique creation, filled with wonder and awe. You have approached even the smallest details with excellence; Your works are wonderful; I carry this knowledge deep within my soul.
PSALM 139:14 VOICE

51
Through the Darkness

God, scripture reminds me that because You are by my side, there's no reason for worry to take hold. I don't have to fear the darkness since I'm held by You. And regardless of the unknown ahead, I won't walk into it alone. I can release every anxious thought as I follow the path You've carved out for me. I can be bold because I am fully loved and protected. You make it so.

Even when the way goes through Death Valley, I'm not afraid when you walk at my side. Your trusty shepherd's crook makes me feel secure.
PSALM 23:4 MSG

52
Always with You

God, what a relief to know that no matter where I go You are with me. There's nothing I can do to remove Your presence from my life. So when I'm feeling isolated and abandoned, the reality is that I'm not. I may be lacking worldly community, but never Your divine company. Thanks for always knowing exactly what I need. My heart is at peace because I have You by my side.

If I ride the wings of the morning, if I dwell by the farthest oceans, even there your hand will guide me, and your strength will support me.
PSALM 139:9–10 NLT

53
In the Day of Fear

God, I admit that I am afraid today. There are so many things that could go wrong. There are twists and turns ahead that I cannot control. I see several outcomes—and they all feel destabilizing. Rather than standing in faith, I'm crumbling under the weight of fear. Strengthen me. Take my anxiousness away and replace it with unmovable trust in who You are and what You promise to do.

But when I am afraid, I will put my trust in you.
PSALM 56:3 NLT

54
God Is Intimately Aware!

God, my heart longs to be seen and known. I want to be celebrated and cherished. But it seems like a far-off hope that won't come to pass. What a treat to read today's verse because it encourages me in spades! To know You're intimately aware of me delights those lonely places inside. You know my heart, You know my words, You know my next step. I am not alone! You are with me always!

You see me when I travel and when I rest at home. You know everything I do. You know what I am going to say even before I say it, Lord.
PSALM 139:3–4 NLT

55
The Inner Calm

God, I admit You are not always the controlling factor in my heart. Sometimes it's my difficult circumstances. Or it may even be unrealistic expectations set for me or others. But I want to change that. Be the inner calm that erases every worry that threatens peace.

Let the peace of Christ [the inner calm of one who walks daily with Him] be the controlling factor in your hearts [deciding and settling questions that arise].
COLOSSIANS 3:15 AMP

56
The Courage to Be a Doer

God, the Word says to be a doer and not only a hearer. It's hard to walk that out when I close myself off from community. I struggle to feel good about who I am, which keeps me from confidently engaging with others. What if I'm rejected as I try to love? What if I'm judged for speaking truth? Sometimes it just feels safer to be alone. Please give me courage to be a doer. I need Your help.

You must be doers of the word and not only hearers who mislead themselves. Those who hear but don't do the word are like those who look at their faces in a mirror. They look at themselves, walk away, and immediately forget what they were like.
JAMES 1:22–24 CEB

57
God's Tangible Presence

God, create in me an awareness that You are my Lord of peace! Let Your presence be tangible. I'm drowning in worry today and struggling to keep hope alive in my heart. Every road feels like a dead end. I'm asking You to pour peace into every circumstance, so I feel it bringing relief in every way.

Now may the Lord of peace himself give you his peace at all times and in every situation. The Lord be with you all.
2 Thessalonians 3:16 nlt

58
Count It as Joy?

God, Your Word says to consider every test and trial as an occasion for joy. And if true, it means I should ask You to reveal the bigger picture when I feel alone because it's an opportunity for growth and maturity. Rather than sit and sulk, I want perspective. Give me Your strength and joy to infiltrate the loneliness. And help me remember that You'll never leave nor forsake me, so I'm never actually alone!

My brothers and sisters, think of the various tests you encounter as occasions for joy. After all, you know that the testing of your faith produces endurance. Let this endurance complete its work so that you may be fully mature, complete, and lacking in nothing.
JAMES 1:2–4 CEB

59
Faith over Fear

God, when I find myself worrying about opposition, remind me of the awesome power Your presence brings into the mix. It's unlike anything the world can offer. And no matter how I may try at times, I can't shake You off. Your promise to never leave nor forsake me holds firm without fail. It's because of this great love that my faith will always prevail over any fear or anxious thought.

What shall we say about such wonderful things as these? If God is for us, who can ever be against us?
ROMANS 8:31 NLT

60
Yes, You Belong!

God, today's verse is such an awesome reminder that I belong. I have a place in the body of Christ and am a vital part of something meaningful. When I forget that truth is when loneliness really sets in. So please bring this powerful fact to my mind when I begin to entertain the thought that I don't fit in anywhere. The reality is that I do. Even more, I'm a unique and unmatched part of Your body!

*All of you together are Christ's body,
and each of you is a part of it.*
1 Corinthians 12:27 nlt

61
Encouraged, Confident, and Bold

God, thank You for choosing to be my helper when life feels too big. Thank You for surrounding me on all sides, emboldening me to live with hope. Thank You for giving me confidence in knowing worrisome moments have no power over my mood or outlook. And thank You for encouraging me to live in the freedom of Jesus rather than the bondage of mankind. Today, my heart is full.

So we take comfort and are encouraged and confidently and boldly say, The Lord is my Helper; I will not be seized with alarm [I will not fear or dread or be terrified]. What can man do to me?
Hebrews 13:6 ampc

62
Purposeful Separation

God, sometimes the best thing I can do is separate myself from a situation. When it's all hitting the fan and tempers are flaring, give me wisdom and courage to know when to take a step back. It may feel lonely to do so, but there are times when we all need space to process. Help me remember that this loneliness is temporary and necessary. And meet me in the isolation so I know You're with me.

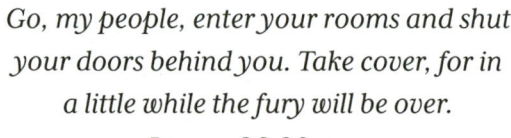

Go, my people, enter your rooms and shut your doors behind you. Take cover, for in a little while the fury will be over.
ISAIAH 26:20 CEB

63
The Divine Connection

God, I see the connection between perseverance and peace—between confidence and calm. I am beginning to understand the payoff of faithful dedication. The more I spend time with You, be it in the Word or in prayer, the easier it will be to release every worry or fear. I won't cling to them with all my might and obsess over hard things. Instead, I will live in perfect peace with You.

You will keep the peace, a perfect peace, for all who trust in You, for those who dedicate their hearts and minds to You.
ISAIAH 26:3 VOICE

64
Isolation in Marriage

God, when I feel lonely in my marriage and isolated from sharing our struggles with others, remind me that I have You to talk to. Be my companion through the valleys. Infuse my heart with Your grace so I can stay engaged in my marriage as we try to work through the differences we're facing. Replace my weakness with Your strength and fill me with hope. And saturate the emptiness with Your goodness.

He said to me, "My grace is enough for you, because power is made perfect in weakness." So I'll gladly spend my time bragging about my weaknesses so that Christ's power can rest on me.
2 Corinthians 12:9 ceb

65
There's No Distance

God, sometimes You feel so far away. I worry that my prayers are out of reach, like they're bouncing off the ceiling instead of reaching to the heavens. Is my season of sinning causing the separation? Is my independent streak making You turn Your back? But then scripture reminds me nothing can separate us. That glorious truth encourages me to check my position, making certain I'm not the one who's turned away.

No power in the sky above or in the earth below—indeed, nothing in all creation will ever be able to separate us from the love of God that is revealed in Christ Jesus our Lord.
ROMANS 8:39 NLT

66
Never Really Alone

God, I would rather feel a little lonely as I stand for what's right than surround myself with people who are bad influences. I know that You promise to never leave me. So in those *alone* seasons of life, the truth is that I am not. You are with me always no matter what! And that means I can use good and sound judgment as I decide whom I will invest my time in.

Do not be so deceived and misled! Evil companionships (communion, associations) corrupt and deprave good manners and morals and character.
1 Corinthians 15:33 ampc

67
God Didn't Author Fear

God, You are not the author of fear. Any worry I'm facing doesn't come from You. Scripture is clear on that. Instead, I was given discernment and self-control. Through them, I'm able to recognize when I'm operating from the flesh rather than faith. Today, help me embrace these gifts so I don't allow anxious thoughts to take over. I want to thrive with a calm, well-balanced mind, just like You intended it to be.

For God did not give us a spirit of timidity or cowardice or fear, but [He has given us a spirit] of power and of love and of sound judgment and personal discipline [abilities that result in a calm, well-balanced mind and self-control].
2 Timothy 1:7 amp

68
Keeping Good Company

God, I know the importance of hanging out with the right people. The solution to my loneliness isn't filling the emptiness unwisely. Instead, I need to make good choices with the company I keep. Give me discernment to know whom to spend time with and whom to avoid. This isn't me being full of judgment, but rather me choosing to surround myself with those who will help me live and love well.

People will be selfish and love money. They will be the kind of people who brag and who are proud. They will slander others, and they will be disobedient to their parents. They will be ungrateful, unholy, unloving, contrary, and critical. They will be without self-control and brutal, and they won't love what is good.
2 Timothy 3:2–3 ceb

69
Cascading Love

God, when my heart is troubled, let me instead focus my mind on Your love for me. Let me remember that it's Your perfect love that can completely cast out all fear. I may be overwhelmed with worry and paralyzed by anxiety for a moment, but when I shift my attention to You. . .all that changes. The negatives fall away. Lord, You are why every worrisome thought will lose its power.

And this hope will not lead to disappointment. For we know how dearly God loves us, because he has given us the Holy Spirit to fill our hearts with his love.
ROMANS 5:5 NLT

70
Putting Yourself Out There Again

God, give me confidence to put myself out there again. I know it's important that I connect with community because it's one of the best ways to encourage and inspire one another. I need this as do those around me. And when I hide away, we all miss the goodness that friendship brings. Embolden me to reach out to others. Empower me with bravery to be myself. And open my heart to new friends and situations.

Let us consider how to inspire each other to greater love and to righteous deeds, not forgetting to gather as a community, as some have forgotten, but encouraging each other, especially as the day of His return approaches.
HEBREWS 10:24–25 VOICE

71

The Most Important Thing

God, I love how Jesus brought His heavenly perspective to Martha and showed her what was important. I confess I often throw myself into work or home and end up overwhelmed by it all. I keep score and feel sorry for myself. Or I worry that I'm missing out on something because I'm stuck. Help me remember that You are the most important thing and that my ultimate attention should be on You above the rest.

But the Lord replied to her, "Martha, Martha, you are worried and bothered and anxious about so many things; but only one thing is necessary, for Mary has chosen the good part [that which is to her advantage], which will not be taken away from her."
LUKE 10:41–42 AMP

72
When You Self-Isolate

God, I'm struggling with wanting to isolate because I don't want to burden anyone with my stuff. So often I feel like I need to handle things on my own. I worry about inconveniencing others or being judged. It's not that I don't want community or that I only care about myself, but more because I lack confidence. Help me remember that friends and family are a gift, and we are meant to help one another.

Unfriendly people care only about themselves;
they lash out at common sense.
PROVERBS 18:1 NLT

73
Holding My Hand

God, knowing You're holding my hand gives me peace to get through each stressful day. It builds my confidence to stay strong and work through each worrisome issue. It makes me brave, trusting that You will both lead my steps forward and back me up. There's no reason to sit in apprehension, allowing anxious thoughts to rule over me. Instead, help me hear Your still, small voice bringing reassurance to my weary heart.

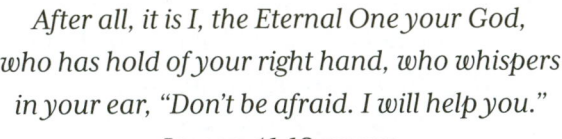

*After all, it is I, the Eternal One your God,
who has hold of your right hand, who whispers
in your ear, "Don't be afraid. I will help you."*
ISAIAH 41:13 VOICE

74
Replenishing from Rejection

God, it refreshes my soul to draw near to You. When I'm feeling rejected or abandoned at work, I look forward to coming home to connect with You. It gives me something to look forward to after a rough day, and it replaces those lonely feelings with hope. Your presence fills my love bucket so I can navigate the workplace once again. Thank You for being my refuge and safe place. I couldn't do it without You!

But it is good for me to draw near to God; I have put my trust in the Lord God and made Him my refuge, that I may tell of all Your works.
PSALM 73:28 AMPC

75
Why Hardship Won't Win

God, keep me from the idea that as a believer, trials and tribulations should pass me by. Don't let me fall into the mindset that life should be easy because of faith. Instead, let me remember that You are the reason why life can't beat me. You're why I'm able to weather every storm that comes my way. Worry is a wasted emotion, especially because You give perfect peace to those who love You. And I love You!

I have told you these things, so that in Me you may have [perfect] peace and confidence. In the world you have tribulation and trials and distress and frustration; but be of good cheer [take courage; be confident, certain, undaunted]! For I have overcome the world. [I have deprived it of power to harm you and have conquered it for you.]
JOHN 16:33 AMPC

76
He Never Leaves Your Side

God, when I start counting the number of prayers You've answered, I realize I'm not as alone as I sometimes feel. You have been so faithful to respond to my pleas for help; I can't think of a time You weren't there for me. In those seasons where my human community feels sparse, please remind me that my heavenly Father has never left my side. The revelation of Your faithfulness fills my heart!

*I've thrown myself headlong into your arms—
I'm celebrating your rescue. I'm singing at the top
of my lungs, I'm so full of answered prayers.*
PSALM 13:5–6 MSG

77
My Firm Foundation

God, when I make You my firm foundation, life just makes sense. Doing so enables me to stay confident no matter what comes my way. Trusting in You allows me to hold on to hope for good things to come, even when I find myself wandering in dark valleys. Let this truth ring in my heart today so I'm not inundated by worry, even though life gives me good reason to be.

The fundamental fact of existence is that this trust in God, this faith, is the firm foundation under everything that makes life worth living. It's our handle on what we can't see. The act of faith is what distinguished our ancestors, set them above the crowd.
HEBREWS 11:1–2 MSG

78
Grappling Alone in Grief

God, how much longer will I have to grapple with my grief alone? I've cried out for Your relief, but my heart is still heavy with pain. I have no one to walk me through this heartbreak except You and I'm desperate to hear Your voice. Bring the peace of Jesus. Comfort my anxiousness. Give me strength to not lose hope. And please guide me safely to the other side of grief.

*How long must I struggle with anguish in
my soul, with sorrow in my heart every day?
How long will my enemy have the upper hand?*
PSALM 13:2 NLT

79
The One Who Saves

God, hear my prayers today because I am battling fearful feelings. My worry is deep and wide and covers multiple parts of my life. You know them all, including every detail keeping me stirred up and scared. Rescue me, Lord. Whether it means pulling me from the situation or giving me strength and wisdom to navigate it, please save me. You're the only one who can bring me peace and confidence.

When I needed the Lord, I looked for Him; I called out to Him, and He heard me and responded. He came and rescued me from everything that made me so afraid.
PSALM 34:4 VOICE

80
The Benefit of Isolating with God

God, I'm grateful for the example set by today's verse. It's easy to feel vulnerable when I'm alone, so I never choose to be. Instead, I fill my calendar with people. But I'm learning about the power that comes from being alone with You in prayer. I'm understanding the necessity of isolating with You for restoration. And I am changing my perspective on alone-time because I'm seeing the benefit of it.

Before daybreak the next morning, Jesus got up and went out to an isolated place to pray.
MARK 1:35 NLT

81
Let Him Overwhelm You

God, each time worry tries to creep into my heart, remind me of Your plan to overwhelm my circumstances with Your goodness. The truth is that You're ready to replace every burden with blessings. And because of Your presence, I don't have to be concerned with the details of my circumstances because You'll take care of them all. I am loved. I am protected. And every need will be met in the right ways, at the right time.

God is ready to overwhelm you with more blessings than you could ever imagine so that you'll always be taken care of in every way and you'll have more than enough to share.
2 CORINTHIANS 9:8 VOICE

82
The Precedent of Replacing

God, I need a friend. My bestie walked away from our relationship and I am battling feelings of abandonment. I've been rejected by someone I thought would always be with me. And because You've set a precedent of replacing people of importance, I'm asking You to honor my request. Would You bless me with another good friend? I don't want to walk through life all by myself. Thank You for being faithful to Your children.

"And I will ask the Father, and he will give you another Advocate, who will never leave you."
John 14:16 NLT

83
His Love Overrides Worry

God, the Word says Your plan for me is for a hope and a future, not worry and stress. Living with anxiety daily isn't Your desire for my life. That being said, Lord, let the good work You started in me be brought to completion. I will have hope. I will have a future of faith-filled living. And Your divine love will override any earthly worry the world pushes my way.

The Lord will work out his plans for my life—
for your faithful love, O Lord, endures forever.
Don't abandon me, for you made me.
Psalm 138:8 nlt

84
God Understands

God, it never occurred to me that You would understand the feeling of loneliness. I mean, You're God! But it must have been lonely when Your one and only Son died on the cross. In that moment, the two of You were disconnected. Your closest companion was gone. I'm so grateful there is nothing I can walk through that You haven't experienced. You're so loving and caring, and it's a privilege to be Your child.

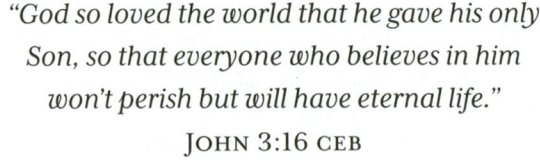

"God so loved the world that he gave his only Son, so that everyone who believes in him won't perish but will have eternal life."
JOHN 3:16 CEB

85
Be Stout and Enduring

God, create in me a heart that is stout and enduring. Make me bold and brave rather than allowing me to be worrisome and wimpy. Let me live in unmovable expectation, waiting for You to intervene in the messy moments. And give me hope and peace so anxiety doesn't invade my mind and ruin my day. Through You, I will live with a beautiful strength and a robust faith. I will anticipate Your goodness every day.

Wait and hope for and expect the Lord; be brave and of good courage and let your heart be stout and enduring. Yes, wait for and hope for and expect the Lord.
PSALM 27:14 AMPC

86
God's Companionship

God, there is no one who can comfort me like You. So often it feels like I have nobody who cares for me in the ways You do. When I look for compassion from those around me, I'm left discouraged because their efforts fall short. I'm not a priority and it's hurtful. But You never disappoint me when I need help. You respond to every tear and plea. And Your companionship means everything to me.

When the upright need help and cry to the Eternal, He hears their cries and rescues them from all of their troubles.
PSALM 34:17 VOICE

87
Encouraging Others

God, let me remember the directive of Isaiah 35:4 when those I love are struggling with anxiety. Let me encourage them by pointing to Your promises to come through. Help me be a voice of hope rather than sit in the pit of despair with them. Allow my words to be of comfort to their worrisome heart. And without fail, let my testimony of Your goodness in my life bring them peace as they wait for You.

Say to those with an anxious and panic-stricken heart, "Be strong, fear not! Indeed, your God will come with vengeance [for the ungodly]; the retribution of God will come, but He will save you."
ISAIAH 35:4 AMP

88
The Good Side of Alone

God, thank You for today's verse that reminds me there are times it's okay to send people away and be alone. It's not being disrespectful or mean-spirited. Instead, it's advocating for myself. There is purpose in alone-time. Help me know when it's important to be part of community and when it's time to retreat. And give me the confidence to do what is best for me so I can be my best for others.

That evening the disciples came to him and said, "This is a remote place, and it's already getting late. Send the crowds away so they can go to the villages and buy food for themselves."
MATTHEW 14:15 NLT

89
When I Wait

God, when I choose to wait on You, Your Word says I will be strengthened and renewed. There is something supernatural that happens each time I surrender my will to Yours, my timing to Your timing. It will create in me a new energy. I won't become weary in the journey. I won't grow tired as I push forward. And rather than worry, concerned I won't be able to make it through, I will thrive in Your peace.

*But those who wait for the L*ORD *[who expect, look for, and hope in Him] will gain new strength and renew their power; they will lift up their wings [and rise up close to God] like eagles [rising toward the sun]; they will run and not become weary, they will walk and not grow tired.*
ISAIAH 40:31 AMP

90
A God Who Understands

God, sometimes it's difficult to speak out about my value system and what beliefs I hold dear. So many people around me believe differently, and I often feel judged for those differences. I get nervous to share my thoughts because I don't want to alienate myself even more. So instead, I stay quiet and alone. Thank You for knowing the depths of my heart and grounding me in truth. I am grateful to always have You.

But you, God, shield me on all sides; you ground my feet, you lift my head high; with all my might I shout up to God, his answers thunder from the holy mountain.
PSALM 3:3–4 MSG

91
When Worry Turns to Anger

God, so often when I become angry, it's my secondary emotion. What's usually underneath it all is an anxious heart. I'm worried about the details or the possible outcomes of difficult circumstances that keep me in a state of chaos. I'm afraid of terrible outcomes and endings. And rather than take my worry to You, I take it out on others. Help me to be aware of this tendency so I learn to go to You first.

*So turn from anger. Don't rage, and don't worry—
these ways frame the doorway to evil.*
PSALM 37:8 VOICE

92
No Place or Space

God, it's good for my heart to know there is no place or space that separates me from You. I can't sin too much to make You leave or work too hard to keep Your attention. You promise to be with me always and I can bank on it. Help me remember this when I feel all alone. Keep my heart from buying into lies of abandonment. Let me feel Your presence in those lonely times.

I can never escape from your Spirit! I can never get away from your presence! If I go up to heaven, you are there; if I go down to the grave, you are there.
PSALM 139:7–8 NLT

93
Where Am I Looking?

God, too often I look to the wrong things for strength. I expect worldly options to empower me in the battle. I choose earthly remedies that end up being empty promises, and I'm left with more worry than before. But the truth is that my strength comes from You alone. You're the one who can settle my spirit and renew my strength. When worry fills me up, let me remember that Your peace will drain it.

I look up to the mountains; does my strength come from mountains? No, my strength comes from God, who made heaven, and earth, and mountains.
Psalm 121:1–2 msg

94
The Emptiness of Grief

God, my heart is full of sadness and my spirit is crushed. I'm grieving the loss of someone I loved very much, and I can't believe they are gone. There is a huge hole in my heart that no one can fill, except You. Please surround me with Your grace and love. Show me the path to healing. Be my companion as I walk this path of mourning. I'm desperate for hope, and I long for Your company.

A heart full of joy and goodness makes a cheerful face, but when a heart is full of sadness the spirit is crushed.
PROVERBS 15:13 AMP

95
The Words Will Come

God, what a beautiful promise You gave in Mark 13:11 to ensure that I will have the right words at the right time. I don't have to be stressed out because Your Holy Spirit will give me what I need. Of course, I can prepare and think through what I may want to share. But in the end, Your words will come to fruition. Let that awesome truth bring me peace and calm my anxious heart.

"When they bring you, betrayed, into court, don't worry about what you'll say. When the time comes, say what's on your heart—the Holy Spirit will make his witness in and through you."
MARK 13:11 MSG

96
The Promises in Separation

God, from the beginning You set me apart and gave me instructions to live a holy life. You didn't ask me to sit in judgment of others, but to instead keep myself from the party atmosphere where bad choices often happen. You promised to meet my needs for community, giving me a place to feel I belong. And while this has been hard at times, You've kept Your word and I am finding connection. Thank You!

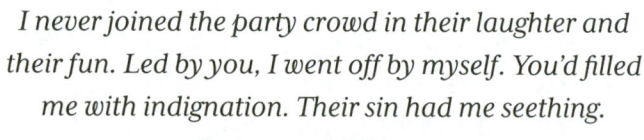

I never joined the party crowd in their laughter and their fun. Led by you, I went off by myself. You'd filled me with indignation. Their sin had me seething.
JEREMIAH 15:17 MSG

97
Standing for Truth

God, sometimes this world feels so hostile. It seems that right is wrong and wrong is right. And it feels like an uphill battle I can't win. But I'm encouraged to learn that Your Word addresses this! It tells me that when I stand for truth, there's a blessing to be had. I don't need to be worried or nervous or frightened because You see it all and will never leave my side.

Even if you should suffer for doing what is right, you will receive a blessing. Don't let them frighten you. Don't be intimidated.
1 PETER 3:14 VOICE

98
Lonely in the Day-to-Day

God, sometimes I feel lonely in the day-to-day, mundane tasks in my life. It's the same thing over and over again. From meal planning to bill paying to calendar keeping, it's easy to lose my purpose and passion. I stop seeking Your direction as I get lost in the humdrum. Your Word says scripture empowers, instructs, corrects, and directs. It breathes new life into old bones. Thank You for being with me and seeing my needs.

All Scripture is inspired by God and is useful to teach us what is true and to make us realize what is wrong in our lives. It corrects us when we are wrong and teaches us to do what is right.
2 Timothy 3:16 nlt

99
Who Cares What They Think?

God, help me not be obsessed with being liked, willing to compromise my morals for approval. I don't need people's acceptance to feel valuable because You tell me I already am. And when I trust in You for my sense of worth, my heart will be protected from unnecessary worry and insecurity. Thank You for that priceless gift, Lord!

*The fear of human opinion disables;
trusting in God protects you from that.*
PROVERBS 29:25 MSG

100
Companionship in Your Calling

God, You designed me with a call on my life, and scripture says I have a hope and a future. I know I'll need Your wisdom and companionship to walk it out because my ability will come from You. What a privilege to journey together! Thank You for knowing it could be lonely, and for filling that gap through the Holy Spirit living in my heart. I look forward to deepening our relationship in new and fresh ways.

"He is the Holy Spirit, who leads into all truth. The world cannot receive him, because it isn't looking for him and doesn't recognize him. But you know him, because he lives with you now and later will be in you."
JOHN 14:17 NLT

101
God Won't Let Me Down

God, You promise to go before me and clear that path as I follow. You won't let me down when I need You the most. You won't ever abandon me to go it alone. So, there's no need for me to give in to fear or insecurity. It's You who I can cling to through every storm.

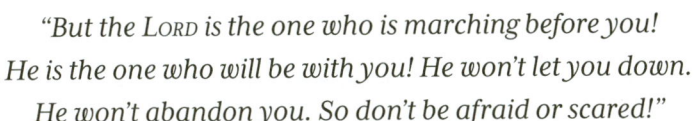

"But the Lord is the one who is marching before you!
He is the one who will be with you! He won't let you down.
He won't abandon you. So don't be afraid or scared!"
Deuteronomy 31:8 ceb

102
When No One Seems to Care

God, I have no one else to comfort me but You. My heart is broken and I'm weary, struggling on so many levels. It seems like no one cares about the battles I've been facing, because my support system has disappeared. I thought I was more loved. Today's verse is spot on for how I'm feeling, and I'm bringing my hurts to You because I know You care. Please wrap Your Daddy arms around me right now.

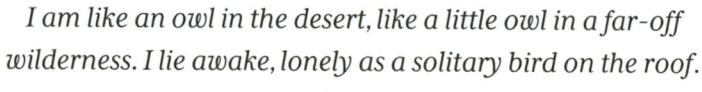

I am like an owl in the desert, like a little owl in a far-off wilderness. I lie awake, lonely as a solitary bird on the roof.
PSALM 102:6–7 NLT

103
Fearing Man over God

God, I confess there are times I'm trapped by the fear of man. I worry about what people think of me. I am stressed by the influence they have in my situations. I'm anxious thinking of possible retribution if I rock the boat. Forgive me for fearing them over You. Today, help me place my trust in You, knowing You're in control and will always protect me. I'm choosing to rely on You alone.

By [the help of] God I will praise His word; on God I lean, rely, and confidently put my trust; I will not fear. What can man, who is flesh, do to me?
PSALM 56:4 AMPC

104
Inflated Feelings of Loneliness

God, when I feel unimportant to others, I tend to detach to avoid the hurt. I disconnect because it makes my heart feel safer. And doing so inflates my feelings of loneliness tenfold. I love that scripture says You've written my name on Your hand. It's a powerful reminder You will never walk away. And even when I feel unloved and unvalued by those around me, I'm thankful to know I matter to You.

"Can a mother forget the infant at her breast, walk away from the baby she bore? But even if mothers forget, I'd never forget you—never. Look, I've written your names on the backs of my hands. The walls you're rebuilding are never out of my sight."
Isaiah 49:15–16 msg

105
The Source of All Hope

God, since You are the source of all hope, will You infuse me with it today? I'm struggling with hopelessness because I'm overcome by worry in so many areas of my life. I can't see past my anxiousness, and I'm crying out, asking Your Holy Spirit to renew my strength and usher in peace. Let me experience joy again. Replace every fear with an abundance of faith in Your goodness manifesting in my life.

I pray that God, the source of all hope, will infuse your lives with an abundance of joy and peace in the midst of your faith so that your hope will overflow through the power of the Holy Spirit.
Romans 15:13 voice

106
Never a Second Thought

God, I love the command to not give those who try to intimidate me a second thought. This is in stark contrast from how I often respond, which is to obsess over them. I get stuck in stress and worry as I try to map out our next interactions. I replay our exchanges. But I don't want to do that anymore. Today, make me brave through faith in Your promise to be with me each day.

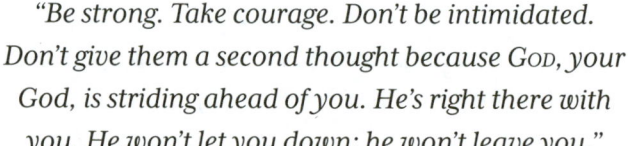

"Be strong. Take courage. Don't be intimidated. Don't give them a second thought because God, your God, is striding ahead of you. He's right there with you. He won't let you down; he won't leave you."
Deuteronomy 31:6 msg

107
Unmet Needs in Motherhood

God, I am struggling as a mom. I'm exhausted and feeling isolated from the things I want to do. It feels like my desires don't matter because everything is centered around the kids. Honestly, most of the time I want to lock myself in the closet and cry. The Word describes You as a shelter and fortress, and I am trusting You to care for and protect my weary heart. Please be with me.

He who takes refuge in the shelter of the Most High will be safe in the shadow of the Almighty. He will say to the Eternal, "My shelter, my mighty fortress, my God, I place all my trust in You."
Psalm 91:1–2 voice

108
How Can I Never?

God, how am I supposed to never let anxiety enter my heart? That feels like a setup for immediate failure. How am I to never worry about my basic needs, especially when this world is a roller-coaster ride? How can I be at peace when money is tight, relationships are strained, and my health is failing? Teach me how to trust You more than what my eyes see. Replace every doubt with faith in Your goodness.

Then, turning to his disciples, Jesus said, "That is why I tell you not to worry about everyday life—whether you have enough food to eat or enough clothes to wear."
LUKE 12:22 NLT

109
When You Can't Trust Anyone Else

God, I feel so betrayed by those I thought cared deeply for me. I feel as though I have no one whom I can trust. My heart is broken and I'm angry, and I need Your comfort. Even more, I'm craving Your presence because I can't trust anyone else right now. The Bible says You're always available when needed. Right now, please flood my heart with comfort, companionship, and peace.

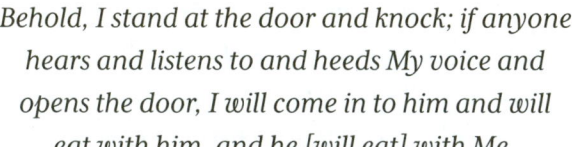

Behold, I stand at the door and knock; if anyone hears and listens to and heeds My voice and opens the door, I will come in to him and will eat with him, and he [will eat] with Me.
REVELATION 3:20 AMPC

110
Using My Words as Tools

God, use my words as healing tools for those overcome by stress and worry. I don't want to encourage their fear but rather challenge them to trust You more. I don't want to join in their pity party or desperate moments but call them higher instead. Let me rise to the occasion and be a blessing in their anxiousness, reminding them to flex their faith so they can stand strong against disappointment and discouragement.

Do not let unwholesome [foul, profane, worthless, vulgar] words ever come out of your mouth, but only such speech as is good for building up others, according to the need and the occasion, so that it will be a blessing to those who hear [you speak].
EPHESIANS 4:29 AMP

111
The Isolation of Guilt

God, the guilt I'm carrying is so heavy. I feel like I'm falling into a deep pit of despair all by myself, too embarrassed to open up and share my struggle. I'm worried about being judged. So what a relief to know You'll keep me from slipping away. You will hold me when I'm ashamed to let others in. You'll bring peace when I need it. And You will remove the guilty feelings that keep me isolated.

If God hadn't been there for me, I never would have made it. The minute I said, "I'm slipping, I'm falling," your love, God, took hold and held me fast. When I was upset and beside myself, you calmed me down and cheered me up.
PSALM 94:17–19 MSG

112
Not Only Hearing

God, let me heed the warning in today's verse. I don't want to hear Your Word and ignore the wisdom found in it. I don't want to let its instruction pass me over. Instead, let Your voice resonate in every area of my life, especially when I'm facing worrisome times. This is when I want scripture to be in my heart and on my tongue with ease. Let my faith yield fruit in every season I face.

"And the one on whom seed was sown among thorns, this is the one who hears the word, but the worries and distractions of the world and the deceitfulness [the superficial pleasures and delight] of riches choke the word, and it yields no fruit."
MATTHEW 13:22 AMP

113
When Church Feels Lonely

God, every Sunday I sit in church and feel completely alone. I've volunteered countless hours and joined small groups, but I don't feel like I belong. I am discouraged to not be more connected and it makes me afraid to put myself out there again. What's wrong with me? You promise hope for the weary, and I'm asking You for help. I need restoration and healing. I need grace for the journey. I need to know I'm lovable.

"Are you tired? Worn out? Burned out on religion? Come to me. Get away with me and you'll recover your life. I'll show you how to take a real rest. Walk with me and work with me—watch how I do it. Learn the unforced rhythms of grace. I won't lay anything heavy or ill-fitting on you. Keep company with me and you'll learn to live freely and lightly."
MATTHEW 11:28–30 MSG

114
Spiritual Security

God, when I have spiritual security in You, worry has no room to take root in my heart. I don't have to entertain thoughts that fill me with anxiety because my faith is anchored in You. Stress can't overwhelm me because there's no place for it to stick. Help me stand strong with this confidence. Let me believe in Your sovereignty. Let me trust in Your goodness. Let my courageousness be embedded in Your promises.

"Blessed [with spiritual security] is the man who believes and trusts in and relies on the Lord and whose hope and confident expectation is the Lord."
JEREMIAH 17:7 AMP

115
When You Want to Hide Out

God, I feel so hopeless. I'm not sure how things will ever work out, and I am worried nothing will change. In my discouragement, I just want to hide out at home. I don't want to connect with community because they don't seem to understand the complexity of my emotions. Would You give me rest? Would You be my companion during this time? Only You can make me whole again and restore my joy.

The Eternal is my shepherd, He cares for me always. He provides me rest in rich, green fields beside streams of refreshing water. He soothes my fears; He makes me whole again, steering me off worn, hard paths to roads where truth and righteousness echo His name.
Psalm 23:1–3 voice

116
There Will Be an End

God, there is such joy found in the revelation that worry will not last. I deeply appreciate knowing that anxiety won't be with me forever. This fear that chokes my peace will eventually come to an end. Thank You for Your willingness not only to take these from me each time I come to You in prayer but also to promise an end that will banish them from ever gripping me again. Today, let me meditate on that glorious vow.

God will wipe away every tear from their eyes; and death shall be no more, neither shall there be anguish (sorrow and mourning) nor grief nor pain any more, for the old conditions and the former order of things have passed away.
REVELATION 21:4 AMPC

117
Loneliness in Your New Normal

God, I'm having a tough time trying to manage my new normal. While others would like to help me, this is something I need to figure out by myself. No one can do it for me. But honestly, there are times when I feel so alone. Your Word says You'll meet my every need. Right now, I desperately need to feel Your presence. I need to know You're in this with me until the end.

Know this: my God will also fill every need you have according to His glorious riches in Jesus the Anointed, our Liberating King.
PHILIPPIANS 4:19 VOICE

118
Liquid Words

God, what a gift to know You understand the story behind every tear that falls. You are the only one who comprehends all they represent. You see the worry that fills them. You recognize the anxious thoughts that fuel them. And You grasp the depth of pain that help them form and fall. Today, encourage my heart to rest in Your great knowledge so I can find a peaceful place in Your presence.

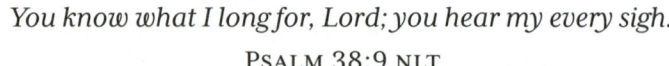

You know what I long for, Lord; you hear my every sigh.
PSALM 38:9 NLT

119
Let God Be Your Home

God, I am at odds with my family right now and it's breaking my heart. I'm trying to advocate for myself and put some healthy boundaries in place, but I'm lonely. Would You be my home? Even knowing my family loves me, it's still a little tricky. With You, though, I always feel good because Your love secures my confidence and self-worth. I feel peaceful and safe. And honestly, it's a refreshing and much-needed change.

When my skin sags and my bones get brittle,
G<small>OD</small> is rock-firm and faithful. Look! Those who left
you are falling apart! Deserters, they'll never be
heard from again. But I'm in the very presence of
God—oh, how refreshing it is! I've made Lord G<small>OD</small>
my home. God, I'm telling the world what you do!
P<small>SALM</small> 73:26–28 <small>MSG</small>

120
Search My Anxious Heart

God, today I'm inviting You to search my anxious heart. I am stirred up and full of worry, but I can't pinpoint the problem. I'm not sure why I'm so unsettled. And my hope is that You will not only see the trouble but relieve the pressure it's causing. I'm struggling to focus in my day, walk out joy, and rest in Your peace. Please meet me in my worry and melt it away with Your love and goodness.

*Search me, O God, and know my heart;
test me and know my anxious thoughts.*
PSALM 139:23 NLT

121
All You Want and Need

God, in those moments where I feel lonely, help me remember that You are all I want and all I really need. Keep me from dwelling on what I don't have, and instead help me to look at all I do have in You. Shift my perspective from victim mentality to being a victor in Your Son, Jesus Christ. And remind me of my value and worth so the enemy can't attack me in those areas that are sometimes vulnerable.

You guide me with your counsel, leading me to a glorious destiny. Whom have I in heaven but you? I desire you more than anything on earth.
PSALM 73:24–25 NLT

122
Never Losing Hope

God, help me stay patient as I wait on Your hand to move in my worrisome circumstances. Let Your Word encourage me to never give up. Let me meditate on Your promise to never disappoint those who place their faith in You. Let the peace of Jesus reign in my heart every day.

Wait patiently for the Lord. Be brave and courageous. Yes, wait patiently for the Lord.
Psalm 27:14 nlt

123
Alone in Your Diagnosis

God, I'm worried about my health and the treatment plan set forth by my doctor. It's scary, and I'm withdrawing from those who love me. Open my heart to let them in, overriding the fear that I will just bog them down with worry. Even more, I really need You. I'm desperate for healing and hope for the future. Surround me with peace as You comfort my anxious heart. Keep me company as I journey down this path.

He lifted me out of the pit of despair, out of the mud and the mire. He set my feet on solid ground and steadied me as I walked along.
Psalm 40:2 nlt

124
Letting God Be God

God, sometimes I panic when anxiety and stress hit, and I'm quick to take the reins and try to fix things myself. I begin to escalate and take matters into my own hands. I'm sorry, Lord. Moving forward, help me surrender every anxious thought to You. For You are God, and I am not.

> *"Be still, and know that I am God! I will be honored by every nation. I will be honored throughout the world."*
> Psalm 46:10 nlt

125
When God Is Silent

God, I'm struggling with faith right now. You promise to always be with me, but You seem distant. I can't hear You over the negative voices. I cry out but You don't respond. How long will You make me wait? I need the comfort and peace only You can provide, but it eludes me. Still, I will trust You. I will choose to believe in Your goodness. In my solitude, strengthen me as I wait.

O Lord, how long will you forget me? Forever?
How long will you look the other way?
Psalm 13:1 nlt

126
God's Presence Stabilizes

God, the psalmist in today's verse didn't let fear win simply because he was fully aware of Your unwavering presence in His life. It was that knowledge alone that steadied his anxious heart. It was knowing that You are unmovable that stabilized him in stressful times. And I realize it can do the same for me right now. Would You allow me to sense Your presence in every worry-filled thought that comes my way?

He is ever present with me; at all times He goes before me. I will not live in fear or abandon my calling because He stands at my right hand.
PSALM 16:8 VOICE

127

Alone on Purpose

God, sometimes I just need to be alone. It's when I connect with You. It's how I regroup. And there are times my spirit craves what only introverting can do for me. Would You affirm that truth in me, so I don't feel guilty when I say no to invitations? Help me advocate for myself when that alone time is necessary for my mental health. And in Your goodness, would You meet me in those times to restore me?

Then, after the crowd had gone, Jesus went up to a mountaintop alone (as He had intended from the start). As evening descended, He stood alone on the mountain, praying.
MATTHEW 14:23 VOICE

128
Embracing the Moments

God, grow in me a greater level of patience as I embrace worrisome moments. It will require me to stand strong and trust You rather than run from tests and hardships. It will challenge me to cling to You rather than work to find my own fixes. But when I do, scripture says I will find joy and my faith will grow. Yes, I will wait for You to bring peace and resolution.

Don't run from tests and hardships, brothers and sisters. As difficult as they are, you will ultimately find joy in them; if you embrace them, your faith will blossom under pressure and teach you true patience as you endure. And true patience brought on by endurance will equip you to complete the long journey and cross the finish line—mature, complete, and wanting nothing.
JAMES 1:2–4 VOICE

129
Separated by Insecurities

God, Your Word says I should be content with myself. That's not easy for me because I don't feel good enough. I've struggled to connect into community in meaningful ways, leaving me with deep insecurities. I want to be liked and surrounded by friends and family, so I try so hard to be what others want. Help me make peace with who You made me to be. Anchor my confidence in how You created me.

So be content with who you are, and don't put on airs. God's strong hand is on you; he'll promote you at the right time. Live carefree before God; he is most careful with you.
1 PETER 5:6–7 MSG

130
God's Wisdom over Worry

God, it's easy for me to worry when I'm not sure what the next right step may be. I don't like feeling confused because it destabilizes me. It's in those moments that I need to ask You for wisdom and discernment. You never intended for me to figure life out on my own. Instead, the plan was for a relationship where You blessed me with what I needed to grow in faith. Rather than worry, I will pray.

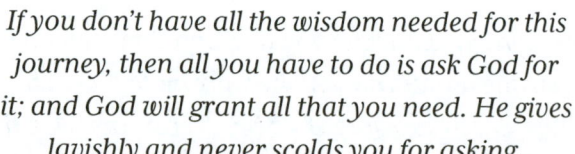

If you don't have all the wisdom needed for this journey, then all you have to do is ask God for it; and God will grant all that you need. He gives lavishly and never scolds you for asking.
JAMES 1:5 VOICE

131
When You Crave Relationships

God, I feel invisible. In a group of people, I feel so alone. Sometimes I wonder if anyone would notice if I was gone. I crave relationships but am nervous to reach out, afraid of being rejected. You know my troubled heart and all the ways I feel unlovable. I am asking You to intervene and grow my confidence. Would You bring me a friend? Would You help me see my value and confirm my worth?

I look for someone to come and help me, but no one gives me a passing thought! No one will help me; no one cares a bit what happens to me.
PSALM 142:4 NLT

132
Holding Up under Trials

God, thank You for the powerful reminder that through faith I can hold up under the weight of stress and worry. I don't have to crumble when life gets messy. I don't have to throw in the towel because I'm feeling overanxious. Instead, I can press into You for help and hope. I can endure as I trust You to bring peace. And I can expect the strength to persevere when I ask for it.

Happy is the person who can hold up under the trials of life. At the right time, he'll know God's sweet approval and will be crowned with life. As God has promised, the crown awaits all who love Him.
JAMES 1:12 VOICE

133
Isolated in Shame

God, I'm self-isolating because of my shame, firmly believing who I am isn't okay. I've done some horrible things in my past that's kept me from forgiving myself. And I'm worried they will keep me from Your love. But then I read in the Bible that nothing—not even shame—can come between us and it provides a glimmer of hope. Would You firm up this truth in my heart so I can thrive in community, unashamed?

For I have every confidence that nothing—not death, life, heavenly messengers, dark spirits, the present, the future, spiritual powers, height, depth, nor any created thing—can come between us and the love of God revealed in the Anointed, Jesus our Lord.
ROMANS 8:38–39 VOICE

134
Made Strong by God

God, when I am overstressed by my circumstances, please remind me of this verse. Remind me that my human condition makes me weak. It sets me up to battle difficulties. I have the tendency to be overcome by insults and persecution. But when I draw strength from You, and Your power is coursing through my veins, I will have the strength I need to permeate and conquer every worry or anxious moment.

So I am well pleased with weaknesses, with insults, with distresses, with persecutions, and with difficulties, for the sake of Christ; for when I am weak [in human strength], then I am strong [truly able, truly powerful, truly drawing from God's strength].
2 CORINTHIANS 12:10 AMP

135
Hiding from Change

God, I am struggling with change in my life. I like predictability and stability, but that's not what I'm dealing with right now. It feels chaotic and makes me want to tuck away and hide because I'm nervous. Rather than ask for help, I navigate it alone. Because You created me and the plans for my life, I'm asking for the peace that comes with it. Help that be a touchstone every time I face unexpected change.

"For I know the plans I have for you," says the Eternal, "plans for peace, not evil, to give you a future and hope—never forget that."
JEREMIAH 29:11 VOICE

136
Never Abandoned

God, I don't have to worry about You abandoning me. There's no need to be anxious that my imperfections will cause You to leave or disown me. Your Word is perfectly clear when it tells me You won't leave or forsake me. And because I pursue righteous living—albeit flawed and messy—Your presence will always be constant in my life. What a relief to know my shortcomings won't cause You to give up on me.

Through my whole life (young and old), I have never witnessed God forsaking those who do right, nor have I seen their children begging for crumbs.
PSALM 37:25 VOICE

137
Speaking Truth

God, it's hard to stand for what's right and speak truth because it often alienates me. It rocks the boat and causes stress and strife. In Your Word, You talk about being with me when I am facing stormy seas and raging rivers. Would You please infuse me with confidence to know I am loved by You and courage to stand in my convictions? I need to know I am not alone.

When you face stormy seas I will be there with you with endurance and calm; you will not be engulfed in raging rivers. If it seems like you're walking through fire with flames licking at your limbs, keep going; you won't be burned.
Isaiah 43:2 voice

138
No Reason to Be Afraid

God, the truth is that I have no one to fear. There's no reason to be afraid. Because You promise to be my source, I can be confident and courageous no matter what comes my way. You will be my refuge. Lord, You will be my stronghold of safety. You'll guide and save me. So let my worries and anxieties melt away as I bask in the power and promise of Your presence.

*The Lord is my Light and my Salvation—
whom shall I fear or dread? The Lord is the Refuge and
Stronghold of my life—of whom shall I be afraid?*
PSALM 27:1 AMPC

139
A Widow's Hope in God

God, I'm in deep grief over the loss of my husband and my heart feels like it's going to burst. For so long, he was a constant companion and now he's gone. Thank You for being a safe place to share my needs. It helps me feel confident that I can safely put my hope in You. And thank You for wanting to hear every one of my prayers because it makes me realize I am not alone.

A widow who is truly needy and all alone puts her hope in God and keeps on going with requests and prayers, night and day.
1 Timothy 5:5 ceb

140
God Screens It

God, what a blessing to understand that You will personally screen the details of every test or trial that comes my way. That builds confidence, knowing that You are fully aware of my limitations. And it keeps me from worrying about if I can come out victorious. You wouldn't let it be any other way. My heart is full and at rest because You have control over my life and will be with me through it.

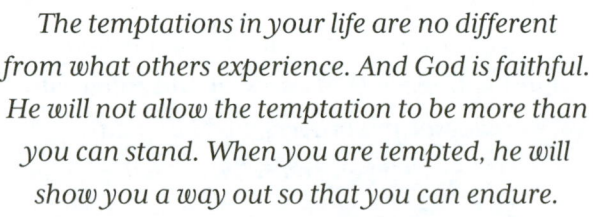

The temptations in your life are no different from what others experience. And God is faithful. He will not allow the temptation to be more than you can stand. When you are tempted, he will show you a way out so that you can endure.
1 Corinthians 10:13 nlt

141
The Isolation of an Empty Nest

God, my heart is aching in this empty nest of a home. I miss having a house full of people I love and it's such an isolating feeling. While I'm glad they have launched and are living their best lives, it doesn't take the loneliness away. Thank You for reminding me I am not alone, because You are with me. You'll fill in the gaps left by others. Together we will figure out a new normal.

Be aware that a time is coming when you will be scattered like seeds. You will return to your own way, and I will be left alone. But I will not be alone, because the Father will be with Me.
JOHN 16:32 VOICE

142
Always Available

God, to know You're available whenever I need You brings great comfort to my anxious heart. I can't always plan when worry will overtake me. Fear doesn't work on a schedule. But to realize I can cry out to You for refuge and help no matter the time of day calms me down. You are my safe and powerful place. You are my proven help. Lord, You are always enough. And You're the one who brings peace.

*God is our refuge and strength,
always ready to help in times of trouble.*
PSALM 46:1 NLT

143
God Understands Your Loneliness

God, it does my heart good to know You can relate to my loneliness. Sometimes it's really hard to open up to others about my struggles because I worry about rejection or judgment. I feel silly and shameful. So thank You for sharing Your feelings in the Bible. It brings comfort knowing I am not alone in my pain. And I appreciate that I don't even have to unpack my feelings. You know because You have felt the same way too.

He was despised and avoided by others; a man who suffered, who knew sickness well. Like someone from whom people hid their faces, he was despised, and we didn't think about him.
Isaiah 53:3 ceb

144
When I Need to Catch My Breath

God, do You hear me crying for help? Can You hear the desperation in my voice? Today, I feel beat up by life. My stress is skyrocketing. I feel exposed. I feel unprotected. And I'm worried I'll be stuck here without You to rescue me. I want to feel Your presence surrounding me right now, in this moment. Let it allow me to catch my breath and find my footing. Let it steady my spirit.

Is anyone crying for help? GOD is listening, ready to rescue you. If your heart is broken, you'll find GOD right there; if you're kicked in the gut, he'll help you catch your breath.
PSALM 34:17–18 MSG

145
Craving His Presence through Divorce

God, I never thought my marriage would end in divorce. I've been left alone and I'm heartbroken. I've tried to comfort myself in unhealthy ways that have left me feeling emptier than before. I need You to strengthen me instead. I need to experience Your presence every minute of every day. Please don't leave me all alone. More than anything, I am asking for Your comfort to make me feel held.

I look up to the mountains; does my strength come from mountains? No, my strength comes from God, who made heaven, and earth, and mountains.
PSALM 121:1–2 MSG

146
When Doubt Creeps In

God, I confess my struggle with doubt, especially when it comes to having faith that You will intervene in my difficulties in meaningful ways. When worry invades my heart, that's when doubt creeps in—often undetected. I begin to work toward my own solutions instead of remembering Your perfect track record in my life. I stop trusting You and take matters into my own hands. Increase my faith so that it trumps my fear—every time.

Jesus immediately reached out and grabbed him. "You have so little faith," Jesus said. "Why did you doubt me?"
MATTHEW 14:31 NLT

147
Comforting the Lonely

God, would You give me the spiritual eyes and ears for the lonely? I know what it feels like to be all alone, and I also know how it encourages a heart to be seen. You've been faithful to comfort me throughout my messy seasons. Let me be that kind of support for others. Equip me to comfort the lonely in their moments of need so they can experience Your love when they need it the most.

He consoles us as we endure the pain and hardship of life so that we may draw from His comfort and share it with others in their own struggles.
2 CORINTHIANS 1:4 VOICE

148
God Will Straighten My Path

God, would You straighten my path today? Anxious thoughts have created unexpected twists and turns, and my mind is spinning as my heart is racing. Help me trust in You. Help me lean on You for guidance rather than following my will and ways. I know peace will follow when I choose to acknowledge Your plan instead. And it will be Your guidance that will allow me to confidently take the next right step in my journey.

Lean on, trust in, and be confident in the Lord with all your heart and mind and do not rely on your own insight or understanding. In all your ways know, recognize, and acknowledge Him, and He will direct and make straight and plain your paths.
PROVERBS 3:5–6 AMPC

149
Look Up!

Come quickly, Lord Jesus. There are so many troubling things I see happening around me, and I feel the groaning pains of this dark world. Yet I trust in Your perfect plan. I will raise my head high and look for You!

"What's happening to the world?" people will wonder. The cosmic order will be destabilized. And then, at that point, they will see the Son of Man coming in a cloud with power and blazing glory. So when the troubles begin, don't be afraid. Look up—raise your head high, because the truth is that your liberation is fast approaching.
Luke 21:26–28 voice

150
Insecurities

God, sometimes insecurities get the best of me, and I want what others have. I want their lives, marriages, homes, or money. But focusing on those things makes me anxious about myself. I worry that I'll never be good enough or have enough. Help me keep in mind that the grass isn't always greener on the other side and that one day, it will wilt. But confidence in Your plan for my life never will.

Don't bother your head with braggarts or wish you could succeed like the wicked. In no time they'll shrivel like grass clippings and wilt like cut flowers in the sun.
PSALM 37:1–2 MSG

151
That Let-Down Feeling

God, I am struggling with people letting me down. I guess I thought I had a caring and compassionate community surrounding me, but I'm realizing I don't. They let me down when I needed them the most, and it's a horribly lonely feeling. I'm relieved to know Your Word says that You're a proven help in times of trouble, always available. Would You surround me right now so I can find peace and comfort in Your company?

God is our shelter and our strength.
When troubles seem near, God is nearer, and
He's ready to help. So why run and hide?
PSALM 46:1 VOICE

152
Setting Your Mind on God

God, when I am focused on earthly things, I watch my stress level increase exponentially. I begin to worry about every outcome and ending. I obsess over tricky circumstances and messy situations, rocked by my inability to control everything. But when I set my mind on You and keep focused on Your goodness, I'm able to thrive in peace. My heart experiences comfort. And my worries melt away as I earnestly trust in You.

Set your mind and keep focused habitually on the things above [the heavenly things], not on things that are on the earth [which have only temporal value].
COLOSSIANS 3:2 AMP

153
Lonely in the Unexpected

God, I admit I didn't see this coming. I was comfortable and secure, but this unexpected change has thrown me, and I have no option but to navigate this on my own. I know You've commanded me to be strong and courageous in times like this. And I know You promise to never leave me to figure it out by myself. Right now, I need reminding. I need to know You are right by my side as I find my way.

"Haven't I commanded you? Strength! Courage! Don't be timid; don't get discouraged. God, your God, is with you every step you take."
JOSHUA 1:9 MSG

154
God's Fortified Presence

God, as my worry increases throughout the day, I long to be covered by You. I crave being hidden in Your great protection. I desire being shielded by Your faithfulness, tucked behind Your fortress of security. When I am, I'll be able to experience the freedom that comes with being unburdened by anxiety. So today, let me bask in Your fortified presence so I can breathe deeply and experience joy.

Like a bird protecting its young, God will cover you with His feathers, will protect you under His great wings; His faithfulness will form a shield around you, a rock-solid wall to protect you.
PSALM 91:4 VOICE

155
Restoring Community

God, thanks for always being for me. Even when I'm wrong or selfish in my ways, You never walk away. Right now I'm feeling a little beat up by some people, and it's a lonely place to be. I know I'm not perfect, but I don't deserve to be ostracized. Help bring healing and give me a willing spirit to work through our differences. You made me for community, so please help restore it.

So what should we say about all of this? If God is on our side, then tell me: whom should we fear?
ROMANS 8:31 VOICE

156
Heavenly Protection

God, to think I have heavenly messengers guarding me brings great comfort to an otherwise anxiety-ridden heart. What a blessing to know You'll keep me safe. That wonderful truth settles my spirit. In those moments I feel the weight of worry, let me look heavenward for help. You're the one who will command angels to defend me in earnest, making it so I don't have to be worried. Instead, I can rest in the promises of protection.

He will command His heavenly messengers to guard you, to keep you safe in every way. They will hold you up in their hands so that you will not crash, or fall, or even graze your foot on a stone.
PSALM 91:11–12 VOICE

157
Battling Temptation Alone

God, so often I feel alone battling temptation. I'm ashamed to share my struggles with community, afraid of being judged. I long for a support group to walk with me, but I'm scared to let anyone in. I know You see the complexity of my heart and have already made a path to freedom. You are so good to me. Would You give me courage to open up to a trusted friend?

Any temptation you face will be nothing new. But God is faithful, and He will not let you be tempted beyond what you can handle. But He always provides a way of escape so that you will be able to endure and keep moving forward.
1 Corinthians 10:13 voice

158
But I Am Safe

God, I don't have to live my life in fear. I don't have to be burdened by apprehension. I'm a believer; my days don't have to be full of anxiety nor my nights with sleeplessness. There is a covering that comes from following You. It's a protection that can't be undone. And I'm choosing to put my trust in You so I can live in peace and comfort. Hard things may come, but I am safe.

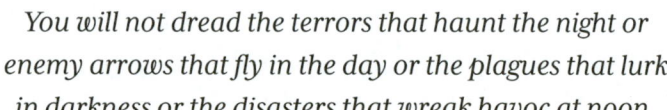

You will not dread the terrors that haunt the night or enemy arrows that fly in the day or the plagues that lurk in darkness or the disasters that wreak havoc at noon.
PSALM 91:5–6 VOICE

159
Financial Outlier

God, sometimes I feel like an outlier because I can't keep up financially with my friends. They have more money and I have to decline invitations based on my budget. Your Word says to be relaxed with what I have and not be obsessed with getting more, but it's hard when my lack of funds keeps me separate. Remind me in those times when I can't participate because of money that Your presence is more than enough.

Don't be obsessed with getting more material things. Be relaxed with what you have. . .God assured us, "I'll never let you down, never walk off and leave you."
Hebrews 13:5 msg

160
An Undistracted Heart

God, I understand the importance of keeping my heart soft. I recognize the value in keeping it tender and compassionate. And my heart needs to stay focused on You so the world can't distract me, especially exposing the tendency I have to worry. The truth is there's no reason for anxiety because You are with me always and everywhere. When I ask, I know You will help me keep my heart sheltered.

So be careful. Guard your hearts. They can be made heavy with moral laxity, with drunkenness, with the hassles of daily life. Then the day I've been telling you about might catch you unaware and trap you.
LUKE 21:34 VOICE

161
Being Alone versus Lonely

God, would You help me remember that sometimes being alone is a good thing? I default to the idea that if I'm not with people all the time, I am lonely. But through scripture, Jesus proved that stealing away to spend time with You is not only good for the soul, but necessary. Give me wisdom to know when I am truly lonely and when being alone is warranted. I don't always know the difference.

*Jesus repeatedly left the crowds, though,
stealing away into the wilderness to pray.*
LUKE 5:16 VOICE

162
A Brief Season

God, sometimes I worry that this season of stress will last forever. The light at the end of the tunnel looks too much like a train, and it worries me. I'm ready to experience freedom from the difficult season I'm having to navigate. I crave comfort and am ready to move on from this place! But scripture not only tells me this suffering will be brief but also that You will restore and strengthen me. In Your hands, I will be okay.

In his kindness God called you to share in his eternal glory by means of Christ Jesus. So after you have suffered a little while, he will restore, support, and strengthen you, and he will place you on a firm foundation.
1 Peter 5:10 nlt

163
Connections in the Workplace

God, help me find connections in my job. I am nervous about making friends and impressing my boss at the same time. I know what it feels like to be an island in an office setting, and I am asking You to connect me in new and fresh ways. Your Word says You march before me, so I am asking that You clear the way for me to be liked and appreciated in my workplace.

"But the Lord is the one who is marching before you! He is the one who will be with you! He won't let you down. He won't abandon you. So don't be afraid or scared!"
Deuteronomy 31:8 ceb

164
Chosen Treasure

God, I don't have to let worry beat me down because I am Your chosen treasure. I am set apart. By faith, I've been called out of the darkness and all it did to keep me in bondage to fear. I'm now in Your light and fully able to experience the power and purpose it gives me. Let me be unafraid so my life broadcasts Your goodness. Let me be unburdened so others can see Your glory.

You are a chosen people. You are royal priests, a holy nation, God's very own possession. As a result, you can show others the goodness of God, for he called you out of the darkness into his wonderful light.
1 PETER 2:9 NLT

165
Joyful Expectation of Friendship

God, I am feeling so isolated these days and desperate for a good friend. There have been many I've enjoyed in the past, but none of them stayed for long. But I am trusting that You have someone in mind, a person who will be perfect for me. Until that time, please fill the emptiness inside of my heart and give me a joyful expectation for the amazing friend who's right around the corner.

Someone with many so-called friends may end up friendless, but a true friend is closer than a brother.
PROVERBS 18:24 VOICE

166
Replacing Worry with Comfort

God, in those times where I feel insecure about myself, remind me that You made me on purpose and for a purpose. I'm not a mistake. I'm not too much or too little. I've been made mysteriously complex by design. Every time I begin to question my worth, replace that worry with comfort. Let me feel Your love squeeze out every anxious thought. And bless me with contentment and cheer at Your creation.

Thank you for making me so wonderfully complex!
Your workmanship is marvelous—how well I know it.
PSALM 139:14 NLT

167
Never Walk Off

God, I'm choosing to trust that You won't walk away from me. I am so imperfect and make bad choices on the regular. Sometimes I worry I will finally do the one thing that makes You give up on me. I know Your Word promises You're with me forever, but I need a reminder today that my bad choices won't drive You away. I can't bear the thought of losing You as my Lord and Savior.

"God, simply because of who he is, is not going to walk off and leave his people. God took delight in making you into his very own people."
1 Samuel 12:22 msg

168
Confidently Trust

God, help me learn to confidently trust in You! As I look back, I see nothing but Your perfect track record in my life. I see those worrisome moments that panned out perfectly. I see anxiety annihilated by Your hand. I have seen Your goodness overwhelm my stressful days and nights, bringing much-needed rest to my spirit. So today, let those God moments be what encourages me to trust You once again in my current circumstances.

I will say of the Lord, He is my Refuge and my Fortress, my God; on Him I lean and rely, and in Him I [confidently] trust!
Psalm 91:2 ampc

169

Loneliness in Doing the Right Thing

God, it's hard to stand up for what's right because it alienates me from others. When they disagree or find me too prudish, they walk away. They desert me. But I want to live a righteous life regardless, and if I have to go it alone at times, then so be it. Will You bolster my confidence and courage, and will You remind me that You'll strengthen me and stand by me in my pursuit?

No one took my side at my first court hearing. Everyone deserted me. I hope that God doesn't hold it against them! But the Lord stood by me and gave me strength, so that the entire message would be preached through me and so all the nations could hear it. I was also rescued from the lion's mouth!
2 Timothy 4:16–17 ceb

170
When God Fights

God, today's scripture doesn't mince words. It issues a clear command to not be afraid because You are battling on my behalf. Sometimes I appreciate a concise reminder to take my anxious thoughts captive. Too often, I let them run wild. I sit in my fear, paralyzed to take the next step forward. But let this remind me there are times You will fight for me, so I don't have to. Give me discernment to know the difference.

"Don't be afraid of them—any of you! The Eternal your God will do the fighting for you."
DEUTERONOMY 3:22 VOICE

171
Feeling Alone in the Battle

God, the battles are so strong right now and I don't have one person standing with me. My friendships are in turmoil, and many have turned away from me. I am scared as I walk out this challenging time alone. I am asking that You come closer so I can feel Your presence and peace. I am full of sorrow and cry out for You to comfort me as only You can.

Quietly turn Your eyes to me and be compassionate toward me because I am lonely and persecuted.
PSALM 25:16 VOICE

172
Keep On Believing

God, I don't usually have trouble trusting You when calamity hits and worry overwhelms me. Going to You in prayer is usually my default button. The problem is that I give up waiting and take matters into my own hands. I jump into fix-it mode. But help me continue believing, even when Your intervention takes longer than my patience. I don't have to live afraid because You have everything under control.

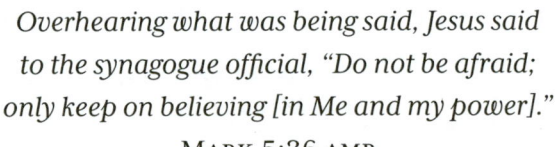

Overhearing what was being said, Jesus said to the synagogue official, "Do not be afraid; only keep on believing [in Me and my power]."
MARK 5:36 AMP

173
Never Separated from God

God, while I may feel separated from others, what a relief to know nothing will come between us. I realize how fragile my human connections can be from time to time, leaving a hole in my heart. So it's a deep sigh of relief to know I'll never be without Your hand in my life. Even when I mess up or try to hide, You see me and love me and promise to never walk away.

So who can separate us? What can come between us and the love of God's Anointed? Can troubles, hardships, persecution, hunger, poverty, danger, or even death? The answer is, absolutely nothing.
ROMANS 8:35 VOICE

174
In the Midst

God, how can I sit under the weight of worry when I see how You celebrate me? How can I wrestle with anxiety when I have You to save me? Why be afraid of condemnation when You promise to make no mention of my forgiven sins again? Why suffer when You sing over me? Help me stand in victory today—unafraid, unburdened, and unoppressed. For Your presence is in the midst of me every day.

The Lord your God is in the midst of you, a Mighty One, a Savior [Who saves]! He will rejoice over you with joy; He will rest [in silent satisfaction] and in His love He will be silent and make no mention [of past sins, or even recall them]; He will exult over you with singing.
ZEPHANIAH 3:17 AMPC

175
He Cares for You

God, I am certain that no matter what season of life I'm in You will take care of me. I'll never be left alone to fend for myself because You promise to meet me right where I am. You promise to comfort those who feel alone, which is me so often. And when I choose to keep my eyes on You and trust Your ways over mine, I can always trust that You will be my Savior and provider.

The True God who inhabits sacred space is a father to the fatherless, a defender of widows. He makes a home for those who are alone. He frees the prisoners and leads them to prosper. Yet those who rebel against Him live in the barren land without His blessings and prosperity.
PSALM 68:5–6 VOICE

176
God Alone

God, it's frustrating to realize I keep making the same mistake over and over again. Your Word reminds me to trust in You over anyone else because You are God and they are not. Situations shift at Your command. Circumstances align at Your direction. Yet, I look toward family, friends, and so-called experts to bail me out. Help my confidence be secure in You to help me navigate the ups and downs of life.

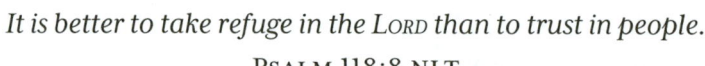

It is better to take refuge in the Lord than to trust in people.
Psalm 118:8 nlt

177
Craving Community

God, thank You for knowing my deepest desires and longings. It does my weary heart so much good to realize I am actually seen and known. And I appreciate that You understand my craving for community. I need people in my life who not only love You, but also want to grow a friendship with me. It's so heavy on my heart right now. Help me trust You'll bring the right people at the right time.

You know what I long for, Lord; you hear my every sigh.
PSALM 38:9 NLT

178
Boldness in Faith

God, make me a courageous woman. Give me a boldness in faith that enables me to withstand whatever stress and strife the world may throw my direction. Increase my confidence so that I'm not a victim of obsessive worrying or anxious thinking. There is no room for them as a believer. And because I know You are *with* me and *for* me, there's nothing that can shake my firm foundation. My hope is—and will always be—in You.

The Eternal is with me, so I will not be afraid of anything.
If God is on my side, how can anyone hurt me?
PSALM 118:6 VOICE

179
The Wound of Rejection

God, I am struggling with rejection. My heart is wounded from people walking out of my life. It makes me feel like a throw-away person, unworthy of love. But the Bible paints a different picture, telling me I am highly valued. It says that You care about my broken heart and promise to heal my pain and comfort my spirit. Thank You for picking up the pieces every time my heart is shattered.

He heals the brokenhearted and binds up their wounds [healing their pain and comforting their sorrow].
PSALM 147:3 AMP

180
Out of Anguish and Pain

God, what a privilege to pray out of my deep anguish and pain. For so long, I thought I needed to be cleaned up before I could come to You. I thought I needed to have it all together. But I'm grateful to know I can come before Your throne in all my fear, stress, and apprehension. I can cry out in my worry. I can call for help from anxious places. And You will rescue me.

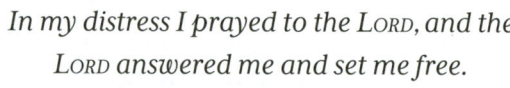

*In my distress I prayed to the Lord, and the
Lord answered me and set me free.*
PSALM 118:5 NLT

181
Always Near

God, it's so rare to find people who will journey with me through the valley of darkness. I know people are busy and have their own lives to live, but I also know You made us for community. Thank You for never being too busy for me. Your love sustains me and pushes loneliness aside. I'm certain that no matter what I'm up against, You will always be near. What a gift and a blessing!

*Even in the unending shadows of death's darkness,
I am not overcome by fear. Because You are
with me in those dark moments, near with Your
protection and guidance, I am comforted.*
PSALM 23:4 VOICE

182
Divine Escape Route

God, there is relief in knowing that You have a clear path of escape planned for me at every turn. You bend an ear toward me, eager to hear what's on my heart. Your presence surrounds me, giving me strength to battle the fears and worries that try to trap me. And You open my eyes to see the path laid bare—the one leading toward perfect peace and provision. Thank You for always making a way.

The messenger of the Eternal God surrounds everyone who walks with Him and is always there to protect and rescue us.
PSALM 34:7 VOICE

183
He Will Take Them

God, in those times where I don't feel like anyone is willing or able to help me navigate the storms of life, I'm so thankful You always are. It's hard to walk these out on my own because they're so emotionally charged. But the Word says I can put every single worry or stress I'm feeling onto Your shoulders because You care for me so deeply. Thanks for not leaving it to me to figure out myself.

*Give all your worries and cares to
God, for he cares about you.*
1 PETER 5:7 NLT

184
Where Is My Faith?

God, knowing all the disciples had witnessed of Jesus' power, as He slept on the boat through the storm, it's humbling to read they were too terrified to wake Him. I confess today's scripture really hits home because it convicts me of my own unbelief. I've seen You calm plenty of storms in my life, yet I still let worry and fear overtake me. Grow my faith to weather anything that threatens to unsettle my spirit.

How can you be so afraid? After all you've seen, where is your faith?
MARK 4:40 VOICE

185
The God of Possible

God, it seems right for me to fear and worry when I am depending on myself for solutions. Every time I put the pressure on me or others to figure things out, it seems normal to battle anxiety because we are flawed. But when I am trusting You for answers, I never have to be uneasy. I don't have to be nervous. With You, *all* things are possible. And Your will shall be done.

*But Jesus looked at them and said, "With people
[as far as it depends on them] it is impossible,
but with God all things are possible."*
MATTHEW 19:26 AMP

186
The Need for Companionship

God, I love that You realized Adam needed a companion. From the very beginning, You created us to be in community because You recognized our desire as humans to belong. Right now, I'm missing companionship. I'm feeling so alone and struggling to feel wanted or appreciated by those around me. Would You bring people into my life who are perfectly suited for me? I trust You to meet that need and fill that void.

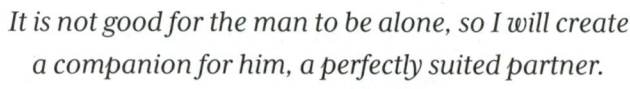

It is not good for the man to be alone, so I will create a companion for him, a perfectly suited partner.
GENESIS 2:18 VOICE

187
The Curative Balm

God, when my spirit is broken, I'm filled with trepidation. I shut down emotionally because I feel a huge sense of dread. And it's hard for me to stay positive as I wait on You because I've been knocked down hard. In those moments, give me a divine perspective so I can lift my eyes in expectation of Your rescue. Be the balm that removes anxiety. And restore the joy I have in You!

A joy-filled heart is curative balm, but a broken spirit hurts all the way to the bone.
PROVERBS 17:22 VOICE

188
Never Abandoned

God, I feel abandoned by those I thought would always have my back. Would You please heal my heart? And Lord, thank You for promising to never walk away from me. Although it's hard sometimes, I'm choosing to believe You'll never abandon me when I need You most. As I look back, I recognize Your perfect track record in my life. So from today forward I will fully and completely trust Your Word.

*You've always been right there for me; don't turn your back on me now. Don't throw me out, don't abandon me; you've always kept the door open. My father and mother walked out and left me, but G*od *took me in.*
PSALM 27:9–10 MSG

189
The Finisher

God, I don't need to worry about how the ending turns out because You're already there. Before my first breath, You planned my life. You blessed me with a calling personally tailored by Your hands. I don't need to stress out or be worried because there's no doubt—You're going to bring it to closure at the right time and in the right way. You will finish Your work in me. My job is to follow Your lead.

There has never been the slightest doubt in my mind that the God who started this great work in you would keep at it and bring it to a flourishing finish on the very day Christ Jesus appears.
Philippians 1:6 msg

190
With You Every Day

God, what a gift to know that no matter what happens in my life You are with me always. When the hard times hit, You'll be by my side as I walk through them. In my grief, fear, anger, and hurt, I can always count on Your presence. And in those times where my family and friends are unavailable, I can rest knowing Your calendar is always clear for me. Thank You for being a constant companion.

"And be sure of this: I am with you always, even to the end of the age."
MATTHEW 28:20 NLT

191
Red Sea Miracle

God, thank You for including the account of the Red Sea miracle in the Bible. While different circumstances, I can understand what it's like to feel trapped where there doesn't appear to be an escape. I know the stress it causes. I have experienced the fear. I know the anxious thoughts that rob me of peace. Today, I'm choosing to trust You will part the sea in my circumstances. I have faith You will fight for me.

Don't be afraid! Stand your ground and witness how the Eternal will rescue you today. Take a good look at the Egyptians, for after today you will never see them again. The Eternal will fight on your behalf while you watch in silence.
EXODUS 14:13–14 VOICE

192
Thrive in Community

God, too often I hide from community because I'm intimidated by those around me, like I'm not good enough to be a part of the group. I struggle to feel like I fit in. Your Word challenges me to be strong and courageous, but that's the last thing I believe about myself. Please build my confidence to reach out and connect. Help me trust that with You by my side, I can create community and thrive in it.

"Be strong. Take courage. Don't be intimidated. Don't give them a second thought because God, your God, is striding ahead of you. He's right there with you. He won't let you down; he won't leave you."
DEUTERONOMY 31:6 MSG

193
Refocusing Thoughts

God, when worries arise, refocus my thoughts on praiseworthy things. I don't want to meditate on what could go wrong. I don't want to get stuck in negative beliefs. Instead, let me fill my mind with what's compelling and true. Let me spotlight the beautiful parts of life. Center my heart on noble reflections. Let me contemplate authenticity and graciousness. Doing so will keep me from an overwhelming sense of fear and worry. And it will bless my day.

Summing it all up, friends, I'd say you'll do best by filling your minds and meditating on things true, noble, reputable, authentic, compelling, gracious— the best, not the worst; the beautiful, not the ugly; things to praise, not things to curse.
PHILIPPIANS 4:8 MSG

194
Not Alone

God, I am so afraid to be alone. It's an empty feeling that follows me around all day and keeps my heart anxious and unsettled. I know You say that You're always here with me, but sometimes I struggle to feel it. Would You please give me the eyes and ears to recognize Your presence in my day? Would You please strengthen me with the bold confidence to believe that I am deeply loved by You?

So don't be afraid. I am here, with you; don't be dismayed, for I am your God. I will strengthen you, help you. I am here with My right hand to make right and to hold you up.
ISAIAH 41:10 VOICE

195
I Can Be Content

God, secure this perspective in my heart today. Let my faith remind me that because of Your presence in my life, I can choose to be content no matter what. Even when I'm stressed or battling fear, I can be happy. I can decide to be emotionally and mentally comfortable knowing You are working all things for my good. Panic, dread, and angst have no power over me when I secure my faith in You.

I can be content in any and every situation through the Anointed One who is my power and strength.
PHILIPPIANS 4:13 VOICE

196
Watching and Listening for God

God, when I feel like no one else will help me, I believe You will. I'm asking You to be tangible in my troubling situation and lead me down the path to freedom. I don't know the right way to go and have no one to guide me. I'm watching and listening for You!

*Take a look around and see—to the right, to the left—
no one is there who cares for me. There's no way out
of here; no one cares about the state of my soul.*
PSALM 142:4 VOICE

197
The Purpose of Friendship

God, I know friends are vital to living a good life. But sometimes I toss them away when conflict arises because I don't want to deal with it. Forgive me! Maybe that's why I find myself alone so much. Your Word says that conflict can be a good thing and is sometimes used to sharpen character. Fill me with grace and perspective so I can deepen friendships to weather every storm.

*In the same way that iron sharpens iron,
a person sharpens the character of his friend.*
PROVERBS 27:17 VOICE

198
Belonging and Being Loved

God, You're my safe place. More than any other person I trust, I am placing my broken heart in Your hands. Replace my loneliness with joy and my hopelessness with peace. Your presence makes me feel like I belong and am fiercely loved.

You are the One I called to, O Eternal One. I said, "You're the only safe place I know; You're all I've got in this world."
PSALM 142:5 VOICE

199
Firm Foundation

God, when my world is lurching out of control, help me and steady me. When my thoughts run wild and I can't seem to get a grip on them, remind me that You have given me a sound mind. I will not become overwhelmed by my circumstances or my thoughts. I will not fear because You are with me.

"When the earth quakes and its people live in turmoil, I am the one who keeps its foundations firm."
PSALM 75:3 NLT

200
The Desire to Belong

God, I have a deep longing to be known and seen. And I want to feel like I belong rather than be invisible. Even more, it would be such a blessing for someone to pursue knowing me. Your Word says all of these desires are met by You. It says You know exactly who I am down to the smallest detail. Let that be enough. And if I find companionship here on earth, let it be icing on the cake.

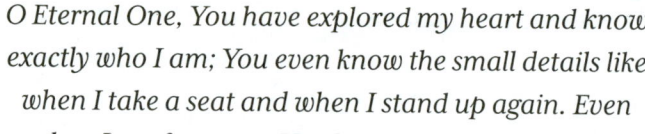

O Eternal One, You have explored my heart and know exactly who I am; You even know the small details like when I take a seat and when I stand up again. Even when I am far away, You know what I'm thinking.
PSALM 139:1–2 VOICE

About the Author

Carey Scott is an author, speaker, and certified biblical life coach who's honest about her walk with the Lord—stumbles, fumbles, and all. With authenticity and humor, she challenges women to be real, not perfect, and reminds them to trust God as their source above all else. Carey lives in Colorado with her two kids who give her plenty of material for writing and speaking. She's surrounded by a wonderful family and group of friends who keep her motivated, real, and humble. You can find her at CareyScott.org.

Strengthen Your Faith by Growing Your Prayer Life

180 Prayers for a Peaceful Spirit

This devotional prayer title packs a powerful dose of inspiration into just-right-sized readings to help you experience the peace of Christ. Each prayer, written specifically for your devotional quiet time, will meet you right where you are—and is complemented by a relevant scripture and question for further thought.

Flexible Casebound / 978-1-63609-895-1

200 Nighttime Prayers for Women

These 200 comforting prayers—written just for you—will soothe your tired soul and usher in peaceful relaxation at bedtime. Each prayer is the perfect way for you to draw closer to the Rest-Giver and hand all the worries and cares of your day over to Him.

Hardback / 978-1-64352-003-2

Find These and More from Barbour Publishing at Your Favorite Bookstore or www.barbourbooks.com